A VILLAGE

Memories of liv _____ *before the age* _, *the motor car*

☙❧

by

DENIS CLUETT
(1907-1986)

☙❧

Edited by The Sampford Peverell Society

Illustrated with contemporary and modern photographs
and with line drawings by residents of the village

A Sampford Peverell Society publication

Published by
Charles Scott-Fox

ISBN: 978-0-9547013-3-8

Printed by
Short Run Press Ltd

Contents

The Cluett family
at the family home: Barrow Hill Stalbridge, Dorset
(Circa 1900)

Standing (L to R): Joseph, Willliam, Alfred, Sidney, Walter (Denis's father)

Seated (L to R): Edwin, Kate (nee Inkpen), Harry, Frederick

Introduction

Earlier this year, the first in the Sampford Peverell Society's series of publications, (a book entitled 'Sampford Peverell: The Village, Church, Chapels and Rectories') was completed, providing a much-needed update to the booklet that had previously been available. The material, and inspiration, for this, the second book in the series, first appeared in the village in the late 1990s when a copy of Denis Cluett's meticulously typed text was circulated amongst a small number of interested people. Realising that these detailed, evocative and beautifully written reminiscences deserved a wider readership, the Society was keen to publish them to mark the centenary of the author's birth.

Our editorial policy has been at all times to preserve the 'integrity' of Denis Cluett's text. However, a small number of minor alterations have been made: these have only been in the interests of readability, the avoidance of the addition of '(sic)' after obviously unintentional typographical errors, or to save adding an abundance of footnotes. Every effort has been made to check factual information with contemporary records and we can confirm that, with the exception of a few minor errors for which corrections have been made or footnotes have been added, the account stands up remarkably well to such scrutiny. However, the reminiscences contain many stories and anecdotes which cannot be checked in this way, and the Society cannot accept responsibility for their accuracy.

To help the reader to understand the language of this bygone age, words shown in *italics* are explained in the Glossary at the back. We have endeavoured to ensure that all photographs (unless otherwise shown) and illustrations are contemporary with the pre-1920 period so that readers can become completely absorbed into this remarkable period of our history.

Peter Bowers
Chairman Sampford Peverell Society
2007

Acknowledgments

When Denis Cluett sat down (we believe some time in the 1970s) to record his reminiscences of growing up in Sampford Peverell, they were intended purely for the entertainment (and presumably enlightenment) of his children, and he would probably have been astonished at the possibility of them reaching a wider audience; we are therefore very grateful to his widow Eileen for allowing us to publish them - and for providing the photographs of Denis and his brother Ray. We would also like to thank two other members of the family: Chris Cluett (grandson of Denis's uncle Frederick) for the 'family' photograph, and Maude Russell (daughter of his half-brother Archie) from whom (by a roundabout route) the text was acquired, and who kindly supplied the photographs of Archie and the teenage Denis.

Although the document reached us in beautifully typed, double-spaced form, requiring very little editing, we felt that, for public consumption, it should be illustrated - not only with contemporary photographs, but with line drawings of some of the large number of (now vanished) domestic utensils, farm implements and forms of transport which Denis so graphically describes. We invited contributions from a number of individuals (all village residents) known to have artistic talents, and the illustration of the book became a Community Project in its own right. In no particular order, we thank Glenys Thomas, Val Weller, Gwen Lucas, Kathy Holmes, Linda Nash, Robin Hazelton, Simon Bartlett and Andy Burns for line drawings (see key below), and Jenny Parsons (for the Map of Sampford Peverell). For the use of archive photographs of the village, our thanks are due to Jenny Holley, Bridget Bernhardt, Roger Greenwood, Simon Bartlett and Peter Bowers. Peter also took the 'present-day' photographs, including that of Trucklegate Cottage, now occupied by Annabelle Adcock, whom we thank for permission to publish it.

The more we studied these reminiscences the more we realised that, although he was writing of a time less than a century ago, he really was describing a forgotten way of life, one which the younger reader might need a little help to understand (and the older reader a little help to remember!); and so we decided to include a 'glossary' and to incorporate within the text a few descriptive 'boxes' wherever it seemed appropriate. We also felt it would be useful - and interesting - to enlarge on some of the references (St Boniface Home, for example) in a series of Appendices. All this, of course, needed research and scripting and I am especially grateful for the work done by my fellow members of our editing team: Mary Hennings, Carole Bond, Peter Bowers and Vic Maynard. I thank them too for their patience and good humour during our numerous team meetings.

Our thanks are also extended to: the Governors of Sampford Peverell School - for their permission to include extracts from the School Log Book; Mr Berwick Coates, archivist at West Buckland School – for providing details of Denis Cluett's time there; Judith Elsdon and Bob Lush, curator and archivist respectively of Tiverton Museum of Mid Devon Life – for their invaluable help with various aspects of research connected with the project, and The Children's Society – for providing information and allowing us to publish photographs of St Boniface Home.

Christine Butler and Malcolm Thirsk deserve very special mentions; the former for rising so brilliantly to the challenge of assembling a disparate collection of digitised documents (Denis Cluett's text, footnotes, 'boxes', glossary, appendices, drawings and photographs) into an attractive and coherent whole; the latter for converting her work into a format acceptable to the Printers.

We wish to express our appreciation to The Local Heritage Initiative – a 'small grants' scheme funded by The Heritage Lottery Fund – without whom this publication would not have been possible.

Finally, it gives me great pleasure to take this opportunity of thanking all those other people – in Sampford Peverell and beyond – who have helped us with this project in one way or another. They are too numerous to mention individually, but we would like them to know that their interest, support and encouragement have been very much appreciated.

Allan Weller
(Chief Editor)

KEY TO 'AUTHORSHIP' OF LINE DRAWINGS

Artist	Figure numbers
Andy	44
Glenys	8, 26, 60
Gwen	5, 46, 51
Kathy	16, 17, 42, 49, 55, 59, 63
Linda	4, 13, 27, 50, 52
Robin	7, 12, 23, 62, 65
Simon	9, 43
Val	6, 10, 11, 20, 36, 37, 38, 39

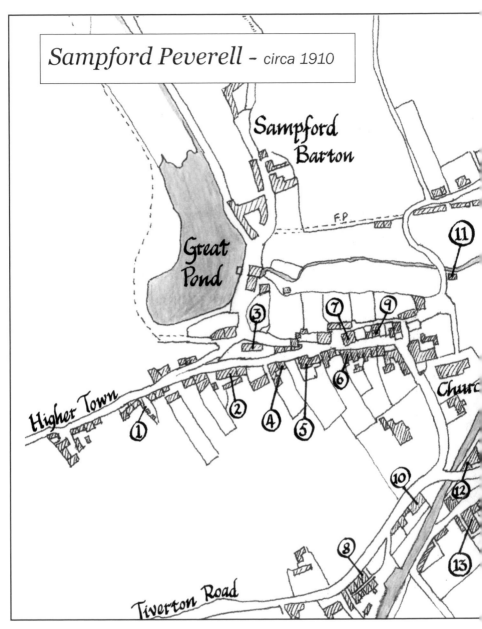

Sampford Peverell - circa 1910

1. Jim & Ann Milton's Cottage*
2. "New Inn"
3. Wesleyan Chapel
4. Baker - Charles Thomas
5. School
6. General Stores - Holloway
7. Cobbler - William ("Cocky") Dunn
8. "Tyrella"
9. Butcher - James Salter
10. Saddler - Henry ("Harry") Wood
11. Slaughterhouse
12. Post Office

*One of a group known as Norrish's Cottages

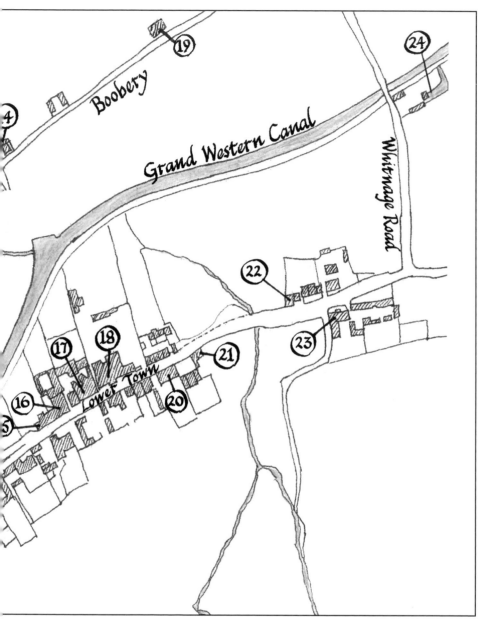

13. R.S. Norrish & Sons
14. "Roberts Cottage"
15. General Stores - Taudevin
16. Butcher - W. J. Williams
17. "Globe Inn"
18. St Boniface Home

19. William Church/John Thomas
20. "Hare & Hounds Inn"
21. General Stores - Jennings
22. Blacksmith
23. Doctor - P. Macdonald
24. Swimming Pool

Frontispiece - The author aged about 12 (circa 1919)

Chapter 1

Sampford Peverell

The small mid-Devon village of Sampford Peverell had about two hundred to two hundred and fifty inhabitants when I was a child[1]. It is situated about one mile off the main Taunton to Exeter road. The nearest town is Tiverton, about five miles away. The village is neatly bisected by a canal - the Grand Western Canal - which runs from Tiverton to Westleigh, about three miles to the east of Sampford. The canal had originally been designed to link up with the Bridgwater & Taunton Canal but the coming of the railways had put an end to that project. The only traffic on the canal was carried by means of iron barges, towed by horses. These were loaded with stone from quarries at Westleigh (fig. 1) and taken to Tiverton where the stone was used for road making and repairing. The two parts of the village were connected by a road bridge over the canal and were known as Higher Town and Lower Town.

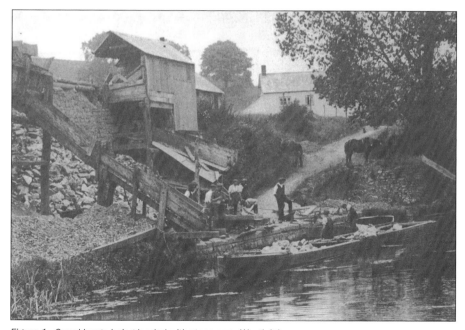

Figure 1. Canal barge being loaded with stone near Westleigh

To the west and north, the village was sheltered by hills, but to the east and south there was flat open country. Twenty miles to the south was the coast of South

1 The 1911 Census shows 613 inhabitants in Sampford Peverell Parish

Devon, while to the east one looked out over some nine miles of country to the Blackdown Hills which guarded the Vale of Taunton. High on these hills stood Wellington Monument - a landmark for miles around - and at the western end of the hills was what appeared from the viewpoint of the village to be a small pimple. This pimple was in fact a beacon, built at the time of the Armada for signalling purposes. It was known as *Culmstock Beacon*. It was built of stone and was about eight feet high and six feet in diameter. It was dome shaped with an opening at the top and an aperture at the base. In practice it would be filled with wood and fired to give warning of enemy ships coming up the Channel.

Sampford Peverell was the centre of an agricultural community comprising several large farms and many smallholdings. I suppose the village could claim to be self-sufficient since we could boast two grocers' shops, two butchers, two pubs[1], a church and chapel, a baker, harness maker, blacksmith, paper shop, cobbler, post office and school. There was also a thriving dairy factory[2] of which my father was secretary cum manager. Here they made clotted cream, butter and cheese which were sent to dairy shops all over the country.

Figure 2. St Boniface Home, Lower Town

1. Gregory's Directory (1913) lists three public houses: 'New Inn' (Higher Town), 'Globe' (Lower Town) and 'Hare & Hounds' (Lower Town)]
2. R.S. Norrish & Sons – see Appendix 1

One of the features of the village was a Church of England home for waifs and strays. This was called St Boniface Home (fig. 2 and Appendix 2) and housed sixty boys with a master and matron-in-charge. It was to this village that we came to live when I was about two years old. At the time of his marriage to my mother, my father was an insurance inspector. His home was at Stalbridge in Dorset and he came from a family of four brothers[1]. His father was a jobbing builder and like most of his kind was called upon to make coffins from time to time. I remember both grandparents on my father's side, but in later years, after they had died, we seemed to lose touch with that side of the family. This was probably due to the fact that the brothers left home and ended up in different parts of the country.

When my father met Mother she was a widow with one son - Archibald, always known as Archie. When I was born [5th November 1907] he was seven years my senior; consequently he was always something of a stranger to me. At the age of fourteen he was apprenticed to a firm of agricultural engineers at Tiverton and was

Figure 3. Chains Road (Norrish's Creamery is the tall brick building on right)

only home at weekends. After marriage Mother and Father lived for some little time in the Somerset village of Langport, where I was born. I have no memories of this place because not long after I was born Father got the job of secretary to the

1. There were seven brothers, including Denis's father, Walter – see photograph on page iv

Dairy Company at Sampford Peverell (fig. 3) and we moved there to make our home in a house called Boobery [sic][1]. After about five or six years at Boobery we moved to a much larger house called Tyrella[2]. This was a five-bedroomed house and boasted indoor lavatories, one upstairs and one in the basement. These had to be flushed with buckets of water. This house looked down over the village and had magnificent views of open country to the east and south.

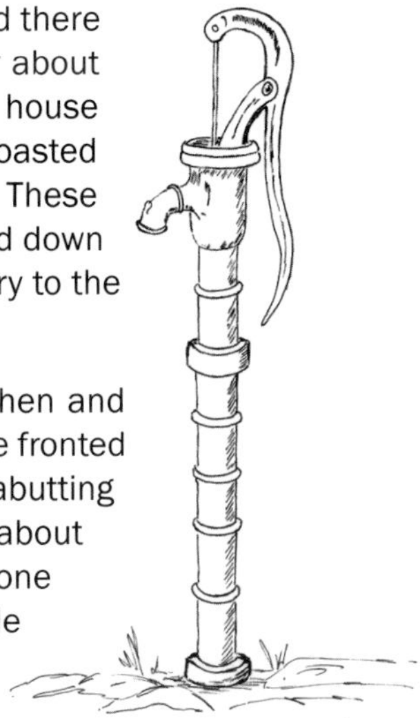

Boobery was a three-bedroomed house with a large kitchen and sitting room and a big *scullery* with a loft above. The house fronted onto a yard and a large garden. At right angles to the front, abutting on one end, was a barn and behind the barn was a field of about two acres accessible from the garden. I imagine that at one time the property was used as a smallholding. In the middle of the front yard was a pump (fig. 4) from which all our fresh water was drawn. In very hot summers this well was apt to run dry and then we had to fetch all our water

Figure 4.

from another pump situated some distance along the lane. *The privy* was situated at the back of the house. It was a 'two-holer': one seat at normal height for adults, and adjoining this seat a much lower one for children. At the rear of the privy was a cesspit. The front of the house was sheltered by a verandah, which was a heaven-sent shelter to play in when the weather was wet.

The kitchen at Boobery, as at Tyrella, was furnished with a large coal-heated *range* upon which all the cooking was done. This range was kept *blackleaded* and polished and, of course, had to be lit every morning before tea could be made and breakfast cooked. The draught through the fire could be regulated by means of a damper. This was a flat iron slide which could be pulled or pushed in or out of the flue. A second damper was provided to control the amount of heat which was drawn to the oven. On the left of the fire grate was a small tank built into the range. This was filled with water - about four gallons - and continuously heated by the fire. At the bottom of the tank there was a brass tap from which the hot water could be drawn. This type of range was common to almost all the houses

Figure 5.

1. Believed to be 'Roberts Cottage' in Boobery – now No. 16 ('Primrose Cottage')
2. Now No. 6 Turnpike – see fig. 57

in the village. Once a week the flue system had to be cleaned and as much soot as possible removed. Special flue brushes mounted on long, flexible wire stems were used for this job. The floor was protected from hot cinders falling from the fire by deep iron *fenders*, usually with a brass rail around the top.

At the time of which I write there were no aluminium cooking utensils - all were made of iron and were extremely heavy to handle, especially large saucepans when filled with liquid. The only exception to iron utensils were kettles. These were often made of copper and were much lighter than the normal iron ones. (fig. 5). There was no gas or electricity in the village[1]. In the evenings we sat by the light of paraffin oil lamps and lit ourselves to bed with candles. The paraffin lamps had to be cleaned every day, the glass chimneys were polished, the wicks trimmed and the oil reservoirs topped up with oil. In some houses

Figure 6.

the lamps were suspended on chains from the ceilings, but we always used table or standard lamps (fig. 6). Not long before the outbreak of the 1914-1918 war, incandescent *mantles* were invented. These were the same as the gas mantles used in gas lamps. They gave a much brighter and whiter light. Special burners had to be used for these.

Bathrooms were unheard of. We children bathed every Friday night in a large galvanised iron tub (fig. 7) in front of the

Figure 7.

kitchen fire, where we were scrubbed from top to toe, usually none too gently. After the scrubbing we were dried and our heads thoroughly examined to make sure we had not picked up any fleas or nits during the week. Before we went to bed we were always dosed with a dessertspoonful of syrup of figs. This usually ensured

that we spent the greater part of Saturday morning sitting on the privy. It was generally held that if a child's bowels were kept open he would not come to much harm. In the days when Mother and Father were children, syrup of figs was not on the market and they were always dosed with brimstone and treacle. When Mother was a child she used to be dosed by my grandmother

BRIMSTONE AND TREACLE
This laxative for children was prepared by mixing an ounce and a half of sulphur and half an ounce of cream of tartar with eight ounces of treacle. The dose varied from a small teaspoonful to a dessertspoonful according to the age of the child.

1. Mains gas came to the village in 1993; electric street lighting arrived in 1930

Grannie Simmons with gunpowder and treacle. After we children had gone to bed Mother and Father took their baths in a hip-bath.This was a peculiar contraption with a high back like an armchair. All water for baths had to be heated in a coal-fired *copper* used for boiling the clothes on washdays.

> **SOMERSET BLUE VINNY CHEESE**
> ......was probably Dorset Blue Vinny, made in the Sherborne valley for hundreds of years until about 1960. It is uncertain whether "Vinny" or "vinney" comes from the old word "vinew" meaning mouldy, or is a corruption of the word "veiny", referring to the blue veins running through the cheese.

My father usually kept a barrel of beer in the scullery and beneath the tap he would stand a large Somerset 'Blue Vinny' cheese. The idea of this was that the drippings of beer from the tap would permeate the cheese and help it to mature. I must say that this method of maturing produced a wonderful cheese. Father always had beer at suppertime. On cold winter nights he would often warm it by heating a poker in the fire until it was red-hot and then plunging it into the glass of beer.

Figure 8.

Father's job at the dairy necessitated his going to Tiverton once a week. There were, of course, no motor cars in the area so he made the journey by pony and trap (fig. 8). I think I must have been about five years old when he conceived the idea of buying a motor cycle. The arrival of this caused a tremendous sensation in the village; no-one had ever seen anything like it before. It was an extremely big and cumbersome machine with a cylindrical petrol tank (fig. 9). It was an awesome sight to see Father set off. He would appear wearing a cloth cap, put on back to front, a pair of goggles on his forehead, his hands encased in huge leather gauntlets and his trousers tucked into knee-length brown leather leggings. In theory, one started the machine by taking a firm grip on the handlebars and pushing it as far as possible. As soon as it started one took a flying leap on to the saddle and away one went. In practice, however, things seldom turned out as simple as this. My father was not a big man and the machine was so heavy that it was a full-time job for him to hold it upright, and almost an impossibility for him to push it fast enough to get it going unless he could arrange a downhill run. As this was not always

Figure 9.

possible the family, passers-by and labourers from the fields were pressed into service to push him. Quite often this meant pushing him for about a quarter of a mile before the machine would decide to start. Sooner or later the engine would fire with a terrific bang and, with a cloud of blue smoke issuing from the exhaust, off he would go, leaving a scattered queue of gasping helpers behind him, while his progress into the distance would be marked by clouds of smoke above the hedgerows and the gradually diminishing sounds of heavy gunfire from the exhaust.

On the whole the motor-cycle was not a success and when something went wrong with it, it languished for many months in the barn since there was no-one in the village who knew anything about engines. It happened that, some time later, a cousin of mine came to stay with us. Percy was apprenticed to a firm of engineers and claimed to know all about internal combustion engines. Sure enough, after a couple of days spent tinkering about with the engine, Percy got the machine to start and decided to make a test run. We saw him off as he made a wobbly disappearance into the distance. We saw no more of Percy until about ten o'clock that night, when he returned weary and footsore. Sadly, he told us that, having got the machine going, he was unable to stop it and it had taken him half way to Exeter before the petrol ran out. Percy had had to walk home and had left the machine in a field. This was the last we ever saw of the motor-cycle; I don't think Father ever bothered to collect it.

My greatest friend was Reggie Russell, the son of a farm labourer who lived a little distance away from us in a cottage along Boobery Lane [sic]. He was about a year older than I was, but we became inseparable friends. We spent all our spare time roaming the lanes and fields and I never remember being bored because there always seemed so much to do in the country. Each season brought its own activity. In the spring the hedgerows were yellow with primroses. We often used to gather great bunches of these. Mother used to send quite a lot of them away to friends and relations who had the misfortune to live 'up country'. 'Up country' was anywhere to the north or east of Sampford, and could be any distance from five miles away to the north of Scotland. Before the last of the primroses began to fade the hedgerow would gradually become covered with blue and white flowers, and in the late spring and summer there were hundreds of wild flowers too numerous to mention. In the summer many of the hedgerows were covered with wild strawberries. Reggie and I knew all the best places for these for miles around.

Early summer was haymaking time and we used to spend whole days in the hayfields armed with large wooden rakes (fig. 10), supposed to be helping the labourers by raking the hay up into heaps. The labourers were always provided with free cider every day of the year. Each morning they would report to the farm and draw their cider which they carried in miniature wooden barrels known as *'firkins'* (fig. 11). These usually held about a quart. If the day was sunny and hot they would leave their firkins beneath a shady tree, and many were the surreptitious nips of sour cider taken by Reggie and myself when no-one was looking.

Late August and early September brought the corn harvest and at this time we used to spend almost all our days in the cornfields. Often we would take sandwiches and have our 'vorenoons' with the labourers. 'Vorenoons' was a snack taken at about 10.30 each morning, when they usually had a bit of bread and cheese and a few well-earned swigs of cider. Harvest time was often a race against the weather. If it was fine the labourers worked from early morning until dusk. When a field of corn was due to be cut the first men on the scene would be the labourers with scythes (fig. 12) who would proceed to cut a path about six feet wide around the field. This was wide enough to allow a mowing machine, known as a 'self-binder' to take the first cut without trampling down any of the corn. These binders cut the corn and automatically bound it into sheaves which were then discharged onto the ground. The binder was followed by labourers who picked up the sheaves and stacked them, ears upwards, into stooks where they were left until they were ready to be 'carried'. For some reason, which I never discovered, the stooks were made with six sheaves for barley and oats and eight sheaves for wheat. When the weather was fine the corn was 'carried' and then stacked into ricks in the stackyard of the farm, where it was left to await the arrival of the threshing machine later in the year. Carrying the corn was often a race against time if rain was in the offing and on these occasions the labourers would work until dark to get the corn in. Many a time I have lain in bed and listened to the labourers walking home along the lane past our house. Often they would be singing 'There's a long, long trail a-winding' or perhaps 'With someone like you, a pal good and true' (Appendix 3). Sometimes I would jump out of bed and peep through the window, watching, as their heavy, ironshod boots struck sparks from the stone roads.

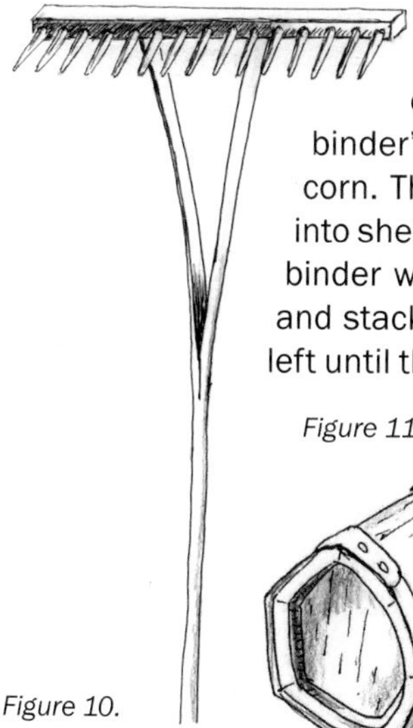

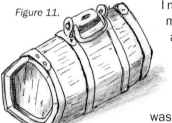

Figure 11.

Figure 10.

After the harvest had been safely carried it was blackberrying time. Reggie and I knew all the best hedges and we would spend most of the time gathering the berries and taking them home where our mothers would throw themselves into an orgy of baking blackberry tarts and pies and making jams and jellies. A little later in the year we would go out gathering sloes and Mother used these for making sloe gin. By the time November arrived the hazelnuts would be ready for picking. We used to gather all we could find of these and sometimes I even managed to save some for Christmas. Round about this time of year Reggie and I used to make a few coppers each by gathering acorns which we used to sell to a smallholder for his pigs. He used to pay us a penny a basket and would take all we could find. The few pence we made from our acorn gathering provided us with the

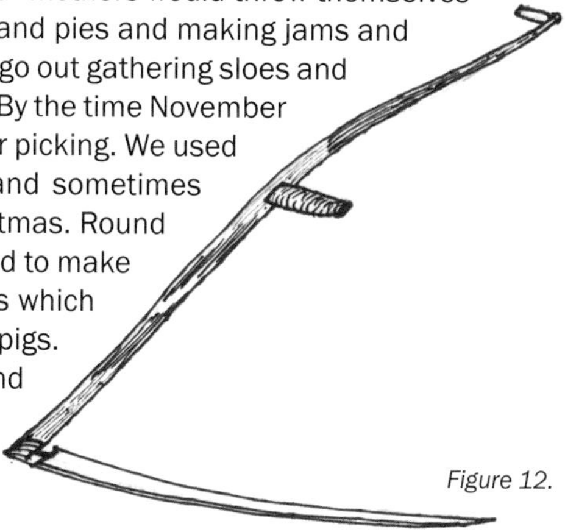

Figure 12.

wherewithal to buy a few fireworks for November 5th. It was possible to buy only four kinds of fireworks at Sampford. These were squibs, which were six a penny, hoppers, cannons - which were outsize squibs, and Catherine wheels. Nevertheless, we seemed to have lots of fun on bonfire night. We always had a good-sized bonfire in the garden. Most of the children would buy painted funny-face cardboard masks at ½d each, and we would wear these as we let off our few fireworks, and ate potatoes which we had baked in the bonfire.

Late summer and autumn was always a busy time for the housewife. Mother made a tremendous amount of jam - plum, plum and apple, blackberry, raspberry, strawberry, blackcurrant, redcurrant, marrow and probably others which I have forgotten about. The fruit and sugar were boiled on the kitchen range in a large iron preserving pan (fig. 13) which must have held a gallon and a half. When the jam had been sufficiently boiled and was ready to set it would be poured into glass jars. When this was quite cold, hot mutton fat was poured onto the top of the jars which sealed off the jam and kept it in good condition. The job was finished by tying a couple of layers of greaseproof paper over the tops of the jars and marking each jar with the type of jam and the date. In addition to the jam, Mother also made chutney and prepared jars of pickled onions and walnuts. Father used to buy green walnuts before the hard shells had formed, and then the whole family was pressed into service to prick the nuts before they were immersed in spiced vinegar. This was a dirty job as each nut had to be pricked all over with a fork and the juice used to stain our hands black.

Figure 13.

As far as the village children were concerned, autumn was conker time. We used to walk miles to collect the best of these. Some of us used to hoard special conkers from the previous year's crop. These would dry and become really hard and, with luck, one might become the proud possessor of a 'sixer', 'tenner' or even a 'twelver', named according to the number of other lads' conkers that were smashed with it. Sometimes we baked conkers in the oven in order to harden them but these were never as successful as ones kept from previous years.

Other games we used to play were marbles, whip and top, hopscotch and 'horses'. Each game was associated with a particular season of the year. I always think of using the whip and top in cold, frosty weather. Marbles and hopscotch were spring and summer games while 'horses' was a game played during the winter. This latter game I suspect was of local origin. One lad, who volunteered to be a horse, would have the ends of a long length of rope attached to each of his arms above the elbows. The rope was used as a pair of reins by his pal, who acted as the driver. We then ran races with other teams. The lad playing the horse was encouraged to prance and rear as much as possible to try and upset the other teams. Some of us used gaily coloured 'reins' which were made of long lengths of wool. We used to make these, by the process known as *'French knitting'*, from bits of wool scrounged from our mothers. This was one of the occupations which we amused ourselves with during the long winter evenings. We also devised many games using cigarette cards of which we were all avid collectors.

Figure 14. Blacksmith's 'shop' Lower Town

Of toys we had very few. I suppose the one toy possessed by almost every child was the hoop. Girls always had wooden hoops which they trundled along with the aid of a stick. All the boys had iron hoops which were made for us by the local blacksmith whose forge was down at the bottom end of the village (fig. 14). I think he charged us one penny for these hoops and would always make us one while we waited. Sometimes we ran hoop races against other boys, but generally we just ran along the roads with them and they were always with us when we had to run errands. Some of us who were probably luckier than most might have a toy pistol which fired caps, but mostly we made our toys ourselves. Ball games were very seldom played by the boys. Some of us did possess rubber balls - about the size of tennis balls - but usually we amused ourselves with these simply by kicking them against the side of a house. Before the war footballs were unknown in the village.

Every self-respecting country boy carried a pocket knife, as indeed did their fathers. Generally these were horn-handled with one big blade, and a vicious-looking pointed spike which was probably supposed to be an implement designed for removing stones from horses' hooves. We always kept our knife blades razor sharp, and they needed to be for they were always in use. With them we cut sticks from hedges and made our whistles, pop guns, catapults, kites, fishing rods and skipping-rope handles. With them we carved out names on tree trunks, gutted fish and rabbits, skinned moles and eels. Our pocket knives were so much a part of us that from force of habit I carried one for many, many years. My father carried one until the day of his death, though he did not have a spike for removing stones from horses' hooves on his; he had a corkscrew. The carrying of pocket knives was almost universal. In those days even ladies carried small penknives in their handbags. Incidentally, these small knives were known as penknives because in the days before steel pen-nibs were invented they were carried and used for cutting *quills* which were used as pens.

Reggie and I often amused ourselves by setting rabbit snares. Between us we owned about half a dozen wire snares and sometimes succeeded in catching the odd rabbit or two. At this time the old-fashioned gin trap was still often used for catching rabbits. This was a spring-loaded trap with vicious toothed jaws. These were usually laid at the entrance to a burrow with the jaws set open and lightly covered with earth. A rabbit, or for that matter any other animal which trod on these traps, released the catch and their legs were caught by the closing jaws. They were horribly cruel things and were later made illegal. Reggie and I disliked these gins intensely as often cats and dogs were caught by them. Whenever we found one we always used to spring it with the aid of a stick and render it harmless. We often used to set mole traps. Moles could be quite a nuisance, especially if they got into the gardens. We never seemed to catch many moles, but when we did we used to skin them and then peg the skins out on a flat board to dry. We always harboured optimistic ideas of selling these skins and making a lot of money, but in this endeavour we seemed always to be disappointed.

Sampford, being the centre of a farming community, was always within easy reach of farmyards and farm barns and these latter were ideal places to play in during wet weather. The farmers and labourers used to tolerate us and never seemed to mind our presence as long as we did no damage or got in their way. Much has been written about the endemic poverty of the farm labourers before the 1914-1918 war, but this did not seem to apply to the men I can remember at Sampford. Their families, and I knew many intimately, always seemed to be warmly clad and well shod, but the characteristic I best remember was their complete lack of envy for people better off than themselves. They were just about the most contented people I have ever known. Most of the labouring families lived in thatched cottages and these were owned and maintained by the farmer for whom they worked (fig. 15). These were known as tied cottages, for which the workers paid sixpence a week rent. They usually consisted of two bedrooms with a large kitchen and adjoining scullery. Their wages before 1914 varied from 7s.6d. to 10s.0d. per week, the latter amount usually being the wage for a skilled man, such as the horseman, cowman or shepherd. These men, who were responsible for the animals, never got a full day off from one year's end to the other. In addition to their wages they were usually allowed up to 1 quart of milk per day. They also had free cider for their refreshment during the day and most of the men used to manage to bring home enough in their firkins to enable them to have a mug of cider for their suppers.

Figure 15. Workmen's cottages in Back Lane

Every labourer had a woodrick. This was a stack of wood built up from gleanings from the farm and its woodlands. I think most of this was gathered when hedges were trimmed or when trees were felled. When trees were cut down the farm hands were allowed to share the wood from the branches, as the timber merchants only bought the tree trunks. Thus, much more wood was burned in the cottage kitchen ranges than coal. Every cottage had a large garden and its own pigsty. The farmhands could buy a newly weaned pig for a shilling and there were very few families who did not keep a pig. All the scraps from the household would be saved, mixed with pigmeal and boiled up as pigfeed. Usually a couple of labourers would arrange together to kill their pigs at different times of the year and when one pig was killed they would have half each. Eggs were quite cheap: sixpence per dozen when they were plentiful, rising perhaps to eightpence per dozen as they became scarcer. Most of the housewives used to preserve eggs when they were plentiful. They did this by putting the fresh eggs in their shells into a large earthenware preserving pan and then covering them with a kind of gelatine mixed with water. This substance was known as 'isinglass' and I imagine it preserved the eggs by sealing the pores of the shells. Anyhow, eggs were preserved for quite long periods by this method.

"WILD RABBITS IN GREAT DEMAND"
Devon and Somerset News 4ᵗʰ March 1915
One result of the war has been to create an exceptional demand in Devonshire for rabbits; never have the trappers been so busy or the farmers had such a rich harvest. Owing to the high price of meat, rabbits are in great demand for food, and thousands weekly are being sent to the Midlands. Rabbits have been very plentiful, but now they are being caught in such numbers that they are very much thinned out. They are fetching 11d. to 1s.0d. each.

Since all the farms were overrun with rabbits, the farmers never minded if their men snared the odd one or two for their own use. At that time there were professional rabbit catchers who would 'rent' the rabbits on a farm for a period of two to three weeks. During this time they would catch as many rabbits as possible and send them off to wholesalers in the towns. While these professionals were operating no-one else was allowed to take rabbits from the farm. We often used to have rabbit for a meal. These were either stuffed and roasted, boiled or stewed or made into a pie. Sometimes we managed to obtain a brace of half-grown rabbits; these would be jointed, covered in breadcrumbs and mustard and fried. This was an exceptionally tasty dish which we knew as 'devilled rabbit'. We could always make the odd penny by selling rabbit skins to a man in the village who made a living by collecting rabbit skins, old clothes, jam jars etc.

As I have previously mentioned, every cottage had a large garden and in these the men used to grow all the vegetables they needed. The farmers allowed each man a certain number of loads of free farmyard manure as long as they loaded and carted it themselves. Many of them had fruit trees in their gardens and most of them grew gooseberries and red and blackcurrants. At gooseberry time most of the cottagers would allow children to go into their gardens and fill their pockets with gooseberries for one halfpenny. During the season I was never without a pocket full of gooseberries of which I was inordinately fond. When we lived at Tyrella we had a very big walled garden but for some reason we never grew gooseberries or currants. I can only think that these were so cheap to buy that they were not worth the trouble of growing. Most of the cottages used to have a strawberry bed in the garden; the strawberries which everyone grew were deep red in colour, rather soft, almost round and about the size of a walnut. They were very sweet and absolutely delicious. We always ate them with clotted cream.

Some cottages had a small patch of garden before the front door where flowers were grown. This was always the woman's domain. None of the men would have dreamed of wasting their time growing flowers. My father was probably the one exception to this rule. He was very fond of flowers and in addition to the cottage garden flowers - Michaelmas daisies, pansies, sweet williams, pinks, primulas and wallflowers - he always grew masses of daffodils and carnations. He was particularly fond of carnations and used to produce them in all sorts of colours and mixtures of colours. He had one huge border completely given over to these flowers and, in addition to our house, which always had vases of carnations in every room, he kept the church and anyone else in the village who wanted them liberally supplied throughout the year.

The farm labourers all dressed in roughly similar clothes. Their trousers were of corduroy of which they normally had two pairs; one pair was worn while the second pair was being washed. Frequent washing soon changed them from their normal colour (brown) and they became almost white.

Figure 16.

Figure 17.

These were always worn with braces and a leather belt and the trouser bottoms were hitched up to boot-top height and secured below the knee with a piece of string or, more usually, by means of a narrow leather knee strap. The flies of these trousers were always concealed by means of a sort of flap sewn on the front of the garment and secured by a button on either hip. In this respect they were of exactly the same pattern as the sailor's bell-bottomed trousers. For the rest they wore a collarless flannel shirt caught at the neck by a brass collar stud, a neckerchief around the neck, an old well-worn waistcoat and jacket, topped off by either a cloth cap (fig. 16) or an ancient bowler (fig. 17). The farm owners usually dressed much the same as their labourers on or about the farm except that they usually wore leather leggings.

Before 1914, rubber Wellington boots were not readily available and the farm men always wore very heavy lace-up leather boots shod with rows of hobnails and steel-tipped at the toes and heels. The laces were strips of leather and the lacing of the boot was carried out by tying a knot at one end of the lace and then threading the other end through the laceholes. When the last lacehole at the top of the boot was reached one had, of course, only a single end of the lace to deal with so it was impossible to tie a normal double-ended knot. In order to secure the lace they tied a peculiar knot in the single end which was known as a pigtail. I have never seen this done since I left the village. The tongues of these boots were about two inches wide and sewn firmly to the uppers inside the boots. When the boots were done up this arrangement of the tongue made them almost watertight and men could work in mud up to their boot-tops without their feet becoming sodden. These boots were always known as 'watertights' and were taken great care of by the men. Every night all mud was carefully removed and they were put in front of the fire to dry. Frequently they were well-greased with either *dubbin* or, more often, goosegrease.

When I went to the village school most of the other boys wore these 'watertights'. To my continual embarrassment I always had to wear a much lighter boot shod only with *Blakey's Boot Protectors*, which seemed to me to be very childish when compared with the rows of hobnails on the other boys' watertights. How I longed for a pair of watertights, but I must have been at school for a full year before Mother and Father yielded to my pleas and I was allowed to order a pair of these wonderful boots from the village cobbler.

The cobbler at Sampford was known as Cocky Dunn. He worked in front of the window of his tiny workshop which opened onto the village street (fig. 18). He was a wizened little man and was always either hammering or sewing leather as if his life depended on the number of nails he could hammer in or the number of stitches he could make in a given time. He never minded if Reggie and I or any other children went into his shop to watch him work, but he seldom engaged in conversation. Actually he was seldom capable of talking because his mouth was usually full of small brass tacks which we knew as *sprigs*. These brass sprigs were used to secure the heavy top sole of the boot to a lighter inner sole which was sewn to the uppers. Hence the expression 'getting down to

> **'GETTING DOWN TO BRASS TACKS'**
> Cockney rhyming slang for 'facts'
> ..... is getting down to business, stopping talking or idling, and concentrating on the matter in hand; getting down to essentials.

Figure 18. Higher Town with Cocky Dunn's shop on the left. (Now 'Halls')

brass tacks'. Cocky would fill his mouth with these and push them out between his teeth one at a time while he hammered them into the sole at a tremendous rate. Once or twice I remember him sneezing when his mouth was full and a shower of sprigs flew into all corners of the shop.

Besides being the village cobbler, Cocky was also the village barber (fig. 19). When we wanted a haircut Cocky would sit us on a wooden stool in the middle of the shop and produce a pair of hand clippers. With these he would go over our heads, shaving us down to the scalp and leaving only a tuft of hair at the front which was known as the *'vorelock'*. This operation was usually completed in about ten seconds flat for which we were charged one penny. Cocky would never have made his fortune as a barber since one of his haircuts lasted the average lad the best part of twelve months.

About a week after I had been measured for my watertights they were ready, and I went to try them on. I can assure you I was the proudest lad in all Devon as I emerged from Cocky's shop with my normal boots slung around my neck by the laces and wearing my brand new watertights complete with hobnails, steel tips and leather laces, secured by the regulation 'pigtail' knots. Actually the boots were so heavy that I could hardly lift my feet so I had to walk by scuffling my feet along the road, my chest swelling with pride as I made the sparks fly from the stones underfoot.

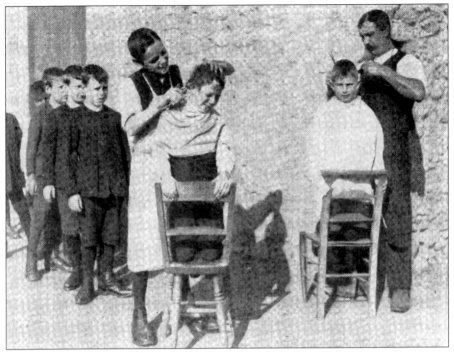

Figure 19. St Boniface Home boys lining up for an 'al fresco' haircut

All the boys and men and most of the girls wore boots. Shoes were worn only by ladies and older girls. Shoes were of the lace-up variety or alternatively secured by a buttoned strap across the instep - I used to wear slippers of this latter style. Buttoned boots were also very commonly worn by ladies. In the towns some men who aspired to fashion wore button boots with cloth tops but these were considered to be rather foppish. A special tool known as a button hook (fig. 20) was used to do up boot and shoe buttons and this was an indispensable item of equipment in every household. We were never allowed to leave the house in the mornings unless our boots were properly cleaned and polished. Since my boots, especially in the winter, were almost completely sodden and caked with mud by the end of the day, I had to scrape them clean every night and put them on the kitchen fender to dry. Every morning I had to see that they were clean and polished before I was allowed to leave the house.

Figure 20.

When I look back to the days I spent in the company of the farm labourers, I am always impressed by the fact that we never heard any dirty talk among them and very little swearing. The only really noteworthy swearing was from a couple of women – Mrs Thomas and Mrs Church – who lived in a pair of semi-detached cottages belonging to the farmer for whom their husbands worked (fig. 21). The husbands were good friends but their wives lived in a continual state of barely concealed open warfare. This may have been due to the fact that while the Churches had about a dozen children[1], the Thomases had none. In addition to this Mrs Thomas was a negress and weighed about 22 stone. Her arms were as thick as the average man's thighs and she was jet black. It appears that, as a young man, Thomas had fought in Africa during the Boer War and had brought her back as a souvenir. The front doors of the cottages were adjacent and one day Reggie and I got hold of a length of rope and tied the handles of their front doors together. We then rapped loudly on both doors simultaneously and smartly retired behind the hedge across the lane to await events. We had not long to wait. Mrs Church was the first to reach her front door and she managed to open it about a foot before it was restrained by the rope. At this moment Mrs Thomas arrived at her door and as she opened it the rope pulled Mrs Church's door shut. Then ensued a terrific tug of war. As each woman pulled her door open it pulled the other one shut. All that could be heard was the banging of the doors punctuated by the most hair-raising profanity from

Figure 21. Cottages in Boobery, homes of the Church and Thomas families

1. William and Florence Church had six children (including one from her previous marriage to Edgar Bowerman, who had died very early in their married life)

the women. At last Mrs Thomas, exerting the full weight of her twenty-two stone gave her door the most tremendous pull. The door handle flew off, the door flew open and Mrs Thomas suddenly found herself flat on her back in the middle of her kitchen. Then, as all hell broke loose, Reggie and I ran for our lives under the cover of the friendly hedge.

One of the greatest attractions for us village children was the canal. On one side ran the narrow towpath while on the other side lay the fields and orchards of the farms. In places the water was bordered by beds of rushes and among these the moorhens made their nests. Hard-boiled moorhens' eggs were considered quite a delicacy by some of the village people and, although Mother and Father never ate them, Reggie and I used to get the eggs by tying a tablespoon on the end of a long stick by means of which we fished the eggs from the nests.

The canal was full of fish - roach, dace, perch, tench and eels. In order to catch the latter we used to set lines in the evenings, leave them there all night and get up to inspect them early in the morning. If we were lucky we might find that we had caught one or two eels, according to the number of nightlines we had set. Mother and Father were very fond of eels, and these were very simply prepared by nailing the eel through the head onto a tree or wooden fence and cutting the skin around just behind the head. One could then strip the skin just like peeling off a glove. They were then gutted, cut up into short lengths and fried. I remember their muddy taste which I always found to be rather pleasant.

For normal fishing we all had fishing rods made from specially selected long sticks cut from the hedges. We usually selected ash for this purpose as it is a good flexible wood and if one was lucky one could find a straight stick six or seven feet long which made an excellent rod. We were able to buy fishing lines and hooks from a little shop at the bottom of the village kept by a slightly eccentric man called Charles Jennings (fig. 22).

Charles' shop was always known as the Paper Shop, since it was he who had the village paper round. In addition to the papers and periodicals he sold sweets, fish-hooks, fishing lines, catapult elastic, penknives, sheets of transfers which we used to decorate the backs of our hands and, in their due season, fireworks, tinsel and Christmas cards. In fact Charles sold almost everything and it was a fair bet that if anyone in the village wanted something that no-one had ever heard of, Charles would rummage around in the back of the shop for about ten minutes and return in triumph with the requirement in a dusty and discarded cardboard box date-stamped 1850. This was my favourite shop and, when I could read, it was here that I spent most of the few pennies which came my way. I used to save up to buy the then well-known boys' papers, the Magnet and the Gem - these were school

Figure 22. Sampford children in their 'Sunday best' for King George V's Coronation (photographed outside Charles Jennings' shop)

stories. Others were small novelettes dealing with the adventures of famous detectives - Sexton Blake and Nelson Lee, with their respective young assistants, Tinker and Nipper. Another favourite amongst these small paperbacks was the Buffalo Bill Library which recounted the adventures of the redoubtable Buffalo Bill shooting it out with the redskins every week. These stories were of course based upon real-life adventures of an American character called William Cody who, when the railways were being taken across that continent, obtained a contract to supply the hundreds of labourers with buffalo meat. He did in fact have many fights with the Indians who resented his success in decimating the great buffalo herds which were the staple food of the Indians. Later in life he started a circus which he brought to England and which was a great success here. However, to return to Charles Jennings, who had nothing whatever in common with Buffalo Bill, I think most of the children loved his shop, not least because Charles was very soft-hearted, and by telling him a hard-luck story we could often persuade him to sell us something for a halfpenny which should have cost a penny.

In addition to his activities engendered by the paper round and shop, Charles was also the village photographer and from time to time was called into service to produce photographs of wedding groups or newly-born children. Once a year he gave a *magic lantern* show in the chapel for the children and as there were no such things as the cinema, radio or television, this was regarded as quite an event (fig. 23). The show was exactly the same every year, as Charles possessed only one set of slides - Queen Victoria's funeral; nevertheless, we always thoroughly enjoyed it. I think the thing which most endeared Charles to the village was his quite unselfconscious habit of riding his bicycle backwards. When he was delivering papers he thought nothing of riding around the village by sitting on the handlebars and pedalling along backwards. He seemed to have developed some sixth sense which enabled him to see exactly where he was going. We often used to watch him as he rode along the canal towpath in this manner and we held our breath in the hopeful anticipation that he would end up in the canal; but he never did, much to our disappointment.

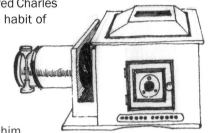

Figure 23.

During the summer, long stretches of the canal were covered in waterlilies and when these were in full bloom the canal was beautiful. I have memories of long, hot, lazy hours sitting in the shade of apple trees in an orchard on the water's edge with my pockets stuffed with green apples and my fishing rod propped beside me as I idly watched my lazy float. Butterflies of every description meandered from flower to flower and dragonflies hovered and darted over the surface, their iridescent wings shattering the sunlight into a thousand rainbows. Sometimes a snake, making hardly a ripple, would swim from one bank to the other. One could hear only the hum of the bees as they foraged for honey or the measured chimes of the church clock as it struck the quarters. I don't remember ever catching many fish, but then, who wants to be bothered catching anything on a summer's afternoon?

There was a man in the village called Joe Barrie who used to gather the waterlilies (fig. 24), box them, and send them off by rail to the town markets. He was a familiar sight leaning over the prow of his boat gathering the lilies while his son, with the towing rope over his shoulder, tramped along the towpath. When Joe was not engaged with his waterlilies he became the village rag and bone man, and it was to him we sold our rabbit-skins, bottles and jam-jars.

By the end of the summer the canal was almost choked by weeds, and in late autumn these were always cleared. This was achieved by two men who gradually worked their way along the whole length of the canal, one on either bank. The weeds were cut with a large flat steel knife about six feet long. This, with a rope attached to either end, was lowered into the water until it rested on the bottom. The two men would then drag it along, using a sawing action. The cut weeds would then float to the surface and were raked to the bank where they were stacked in heaps and left to rot.

Figure 24. The Barrie brothers harvesting water lilies

In winter the canal often froze over and I remember one year, after several days of very hard frost, the canal was frozen throughout its entire length and one could skate into Tiverton. It stayed like this for over a week and the first Saturday and Sunday the ice would 'bear', practically the whole village turned out and pairs of rusty skates appeared as if by magic. Those of us who did not possess skates enjoyed ourselves by sliding. Most of the skates were very primitive by modern standards. They usually consisted of a steel blade inserted into a wooden sole and these were then attached to boots by means of wood screws. It was really extraordinary how many men could skate. Generally none of the women could skate and so they brought wooden chairs onto the ice and, seated on these, they could enjoy themselves by being propelled along by their husbands. Unfortunately our ice revels ended in tragedy when, the following weekend, a little girl fell through the ice and was drowned.

Boobery, although situated outside the mainstream of the village, was continually visited by tramps, gypsies and a varied assortment of itinerants. For this reason we acquired a dog, called Prince. Prince was a bull terrier with a chest like that of a prizefighter, and he was the terror of the district. Nobody ever dared to open our gate if Prince was loose. At the sight of his teeth, which he was never slow to show to strangers, they would stop dead in their tracks. He hated the sight of every living thing, whether on four legs or two, except the family, and all of us he loved without restraint. The main object of his adoration, however, was my father who in Prince's eyes could do no wrong. When he was in the house he would allow no-one to sit in Father's favourite armchair; he would guard this for hours until my father came home and sat down. As soon as Father sat down Prince would trot out to the scullery and fetch his slippers, place them on the hearth-rug and guard them until Father decided to put them on. We used to allow him to sleep in the kitchen during the winter months and he was a wonderful house dog. I remember one night Prince heard prowlers near the house and went straight through the kitchen window after them, smashing the glass into smithereens. When we examined him the next morning he didn't have a scratch on him.

At times he would be affected by wanderlust and he would completely disappear for three or four days at a time. We never found out where he went or what he did. When he returned we would usually discover him one morning lying outside the front door, completely exhausted, with raw pads, covered in mud and blood. We would carry him indoors where he would lap up a bowl of bread and milk and then sleep for perhaps eight or twelve hours at a stretch.

When we first had Prince the *rabies* law was very strictly enforced and dogs were not allowed on the public highway unless they were muzzled. After we'd had him for a couple of years this law was relaxed, as rabies had been stamped out. We eventually had to have Prince put down as he was accused of sheep-worrying. Although we were able to prove in several cases that in fact Prince was not the culprit, we nevertheless had to bow to public opinion in the end. My father was so upset that we never had another dog.

We used to get a lot of tramps passing through the village en route from Tiverton workhouse to the one at Wellington. During the winter months they would work their way around the country from one workhouse to another spending one night in each, and in return for an evening meal, a bed and breakfast they had to do a certain stint of work before they were allowed to move on. The work usually consisted of scrubbing floors, shovelling coal, chopping wood or even cracking stones for road repairs. Most of them hated the workhouse and preferred to sleep rough whenever the weather was amenable.

Usually the tramps were loners but very occasionally one would see one who was accompanied by a woman. They carried all their possessions in bundles slung over their shoulders and invariably wore tattered overcoats summer and winter. They always carried a *billycan* in which they made tea and had a habit of calling at a house to ask for their cans to be filled with boiling water. If they were lucky they would be sent on their way with a can of freshly made tea complete with milk and sugar and often some bread and butter or a slice of cake. If they were refused they seldom argued but simply shrugged their shoulders and went on their way. It was not good policy to be over-generous with these vagrants since they could communicate with each other by scratching signs on the walls or in the roadway or sometimes by an arrangement of stones stuck in the hedgerow. If any particular house got the name of being a 'soft touch' it wasn't long before the news spread among the fraternity and one would be pestered all day and every day.

The most difficult callers to get rid of were the gypsies. These were always womenfolk and arrived at the door carrying a large basket on one arm and frequently a baby on the other, suckling at the mother's breast. In their baskets they carried clothes pegs, which they had made themselves, together with rolls of lace, cards of hooks and eyes, reels of cotton and the like which they tried to sell. If they could not persuade the housewife to buy anything they would try to wheedle food, clothes or money. They all claimed to have pure *Romany* blood and to be adept at reading palms. Many were the country girls and women whom they conned into having their fortunes told after the Romany's hand had been crossed with silver.

The gypsy men never begged and had a wonderful knack of keeping out of sight. When one passed one of their encampments by the roadside one would see them lazing about smoking clay pipes while the grannies of the tribe, also smoking clay pipes, would be preparing and cooking a meal over a fire of sticks. If one ever caught a glimpse of a gypsy man away from the encampment he was usually sidling

Figure 25. Typical picture taken in Sampford Peverell by a travelling photographer: this one is of the Kerslake family

furtively along under the cover of a hedge with a lurcher dog at his heels. Lurchers were a cross between a greyhound and a collie and were wonderful poachers - fast and intelligent. It was believed that they were trained to smell out and take pheasants, partridges, rabbits and hares and even chickens from farmyards in absolute silence. All gypsies were considered to be inveterate thieves and no householder or farmer liked to see their caravans anywhere near their premises. There were many other travellers on the roads besides gypsies and tramps. Travelling tinkers who would mend pots and pans, salesmen on foot carrying a selection of cheap jewellery and trinkets, horse-drawn covered vans hung about both inside and out with pots, pans and kettles of every conceivable size and shape, and knife and scissor grinders who went around the country on tricycles adapted to take a small grindstone on the front which could be worked by the pedals of the machine. Sometimes we were even visited by travelling photographers who would take one's photo and develop and print it on a tin plate while one waited (fig. 25).

Among the more welcome of these itinerants were the Breton onion-sellers (fig. 26). These men used to scour the countryside on bicycles with their persons and machines festooned with strings of onions. Most of them had very little English but seemed to have a good grasp of our coinage system. The advent of one of these men at the door would initiate a long bargaining session as they usually asked about three times as much for a string of onions as they were likely to get.

Figure 26.

I suppose the men who lived the loneliest lives were the roadmen and the stone-crackers. The roadmen, employed by the Council, were each responsible for the upkeep of the roads within a certain area. They spent their days keeping the drains and the ditches clear and ensuring that the hedge-bottoms and verges did not encroach on the highways. At this time there were no tarmacadam road surfaces; they were finished by compacting small pieces of stone into a reasonably smooth surface by means of a steam-roller. In winter the roads were always muddy and full of potholes and in summer they were always very dusty.

The stones used for the repair and surfacing of the roads were prepared by men known as stone-crackers. These men were at the bottom of the labouring hierarchy and spent their lives sitting by the roadside on the grass verge breaking piles of large stones and boulders into small pieces suitable for rolling into the road surface. They piled the broken stones into long heaps, flat on top and with sloping sides and once a week they would be visited by a council surveyor who would measure the heap and would pay them at the rate of a few pence per yard. The pay was abysmally low and a man would have to be on the lowest rung of poverty before taking the job. Like all labourers, these men never wore overcoats. They protected themselves from the cold and rain by tying a sack over their shoulders to protect their backs, and tying a second one around the waist as an apron which protected their thighs. Most of the men

STONE CRACKERS
Devon and Somerset News 26ᵗʰ March 1914
A compensation claim, heard at Tiverton County Court in March 1914, concerned an Uplowman man by the name of Prescott who was employed by Tiverton Rural Council to crack stones on the highway near Sampford Peverell, and who had sustained an injury to his eye when a piece of stone broke through his goggles.

wore goggles to protect their eyes from flying fragments of stone but even so it was no uncommon sight to see one of these men wearing a patch over a blinded eye.

The steam rollers with their teams were hired by the Council from contractors. The team usually consisted of four men and their leader was the engine driver. Since they often had to work some distance away from their houses they were provided with a covered wagon in which they cooked their meals and slept.

A lot of road traffic consisted of a train of one or two trucks drawn by a steam traction engine. Coal, flour, cattlefood, corn and meal, and heavy farm machinery were often collected from the railway sidings and distributed to outlying depots by this means. Breweries also relied a lot upon steam transport to deliver the beer from the town brewery to the village pubs. Tiverton Breweries had a fleet of Foden steam wagons (fig. 27). These were a common sight on the roads, loaded with barrels of beer while the driver and his mate sat in an enclosed cab very much like the modern motor lorry. These vehicles were considered to be very fast as they used to travel at about fifteen miles per hour. Nevertheless, the greater part of the traffic consisted of horse-drawn vehicles.

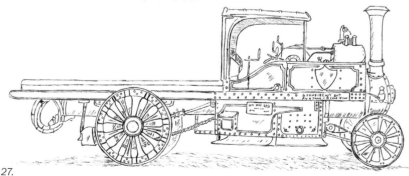

Figure 27.

Chapter 2

Shops

Sampford Peverell was quite well served by shops and I suppose one could buy most everyday requirements within the village. Adjoining the school in Higher Town was a small baker's shop known as Thomas' (fig. 28). Although I suppose most people baked their own bread, the shop was always handy if one wanted yeast cakes or an extra loaf or two. They sold two kinds of loaf - tinned and cottage. I remember we used to buy tinned loaves if we were going on a picnic or having a party since bread for sandwiches could be cut much more easily and tidily from the baker's tinned loaf. They also used to make miniature cottage loaves known as milk loaves, so called because the dough was mixed with milk instead of water. They used to sell these for one farthing and we bought and ate them hot from the oven. They were delicious. The village also relied upon Thomas the baker for their hot cross buns, delivered before breakfast still hot from the oven, on the morning of Good Friday.

Figure 28. Unloading flour at Thomas' bakery, Higher Town

Just below the school, opposite Cocky Dunn's cobbler's shop, was Holloway's store which sold everything from sweets to haberdashery (fig. 29). It was kept by two maiden ladies - the Misses Holloway. It was the children's favourite sweet shop and the two very sweet ladies would cheerfully go to endless trouble to help a child to choose a farthing's worth of sweets. The sweets were kept in large glass jars so

Figure 29. Higher Town, with Holloway's shop on right. (now Cowlings)

that one could always see what was available. One had quite a selection of sweets to choose from, even by today's standards. They included acid drops, pear drops, Rowntree gums, humbugs, gob-stoppers, scented *cachous*, liquorice allsorts, liquorice bootlaces and a particularly hot peppermint known as 'extra strength'. One of our favourite buys was farthing sherbet bags. These consisted of a sealed paper bag containing sherbet with a liquorice tube sticking out at one end through which one sucked the contents. Halfpenny bars of chocolate and chocolate drops were also available and also some small round sweets in varied colours on which were printed mottoes and legends such as 'I love you' and 'Kiss me'. I imagine that the idea of these was that one would buy them and present the girl of one's choice with one carrying a suitable message. Since most of us had very little money to spare I don't remember any great rush to share these sweets with the girls.

At this time the farthing was a coin in constant use. Apart from the fact that one could buy a farthing's worth of sweets, it was used a lot in the haberdashery trade. Many items such as ribbons, elastic, materials etc. were priced by the yard at amounts like 2¾d., 1¾d., 1s.11¾d. etc. If a shopkeeper was short of farthings in his till he would often offer a packet of pins or hairpins instead of an odd farthing in the change. In addition to the farthings, we used the halfpenny, penny, silver threepenny piece, sixpence, shilling, two shilling piece or florin, half crown and five shilling piece or crown. This latter coin was silver and almost half as big again as the half crown. It was very clumsy and rapidly went out of use during the First World War. Before the war the golden sovereign [£1], the golden guinea [£1.1s.0d.] and golden half sovereigns were quite common, as also were one pound and ten shilling notes. It was not uncommon for gentlemen to carry sovereign cases, often attached to one end of their watch chains. These metal cases, often of silver, would hold three or four sovereigns. The coins were slipped one at a time under a rim and held in place by a springloaded metal disc. In 1914 all gold coins were called in by the Treasury and replaced by notes.

Most men carried pocket watches in the left-hand waistcoat pocket on the end of a gold or silver chain. To the other end of the chain was attached the key used for winding the watch and re-setting the hands. The chain was taken across the waistcoat, through a vertical button-hole to the right-hand pocket. Many men wore ornaments such as medals or charms on their watch chains.

There were two butcher's shops in the village, one in Higher Town – Salter's, and one in Lower Town - Williams' (fig. 30). They and the butchers were replicas of each other. Both were kept scrupulously clean, and the floors liberally sprinkled with clean sawdust. The main feature in each, standing in the centre of the shop, was the chopping block - a massive section of a tree trunk. There were no refrigerators and the whole carcasses of the animals were hung around the shop

Figure 30. 'Challis', Lower Town (Williams' butchers) with the Globe Inn beyond

to be laid on the block and chopped up as required. Joints were always sold complete with the bone. The two butchers always dressed alike in snowy white shirts with the sleeves rolled up above the elbows, a blue and white striped apron girt about the waist with a length of thin rope from which hung a selection of knives and a sharpening steel. They both wore breeches with black leggings and boots, both of which were always polished to a mirror finish. The whole ensemble was topped off by a straw boater.

Both butchers slaughtered their own animals. Butcher Salter's slaughterhouse was situated on the bank of a stream some little distance from his shop. During the holidays Reg Russell and I often used to spend a morning watching the animals being slaughtered. Humane killing had not been heard of at this time. Sheep and pigs were killed by the knife, calves were poleaxed and bullocks were shot by a special cartridge fired from a twelve-bore shotgun. On the whole it was a pretty gory business and, as far as the pigs were concerned, a pretty noisy one too. However, we children took it all as a matter of course, and I don't think we were brutalised by something which to us seemed very ordinary and necessary. If we were lucky, Salter would give us a pig's bladder which we could inflate and use as a football.

The main shop in the village was Taudevin's Store, situated in Lower Town (fig.31) and run by a brother and sister with the aid of a middle-aged woman assistant whom Taudevin later married. They sold groceries and haberdashery. Taudevin was a good businessman and ran a delivery service to outlying farms and hamlets in the parish. He used to go around on his bicycle on Wednesdays taking orders which he delivered by horse-drawn van on Saturdays. From his shop one could buy almost anything from lard and cheese to paraffin and candles. He always wore a long white apron, tied around the waist and reaching to his boot-tops. His aprons were never hemmed at the bottom and consequently always had a frayed edge.

Since very few of the commodities were pre-packed, the grocer and his assistant spent a great deal of their time weighing and packing items of an order into paper bags or greaseproof paper. The bags were of three types: white, which was used for flour, bacon, lard, biscuits etc.; blue, used for rice, sugar, tapioca etc., and small triangular white bags for items usually bought by the ounce, such as pepper, sweets, ground ginger etc. Although some manufacturers sold pre-packed tea, quite a lot was sold loose and in the shops it was kept in large canisters decorated with Chinese or Indian pictures and weighed out as the customer required. Frequently the customer would ask for the tea to be blended to suit their own taste. I remember mother used to have her own tea blended from four different teas. The grocer would weigh out the different teas in their correct proportions and then carefully mix them. The resultant blend was never put into a prefabricated

Figure 31. Taudevin's shop on the day of Sampford Fair

paper bag. A square of stout, white paper was placed on the counter and the tea poured into a heap in the centre. This was carefully folded into a neat little parcel and tied with a piece of thin white string.

Vinegar was always sold loose from a barrel, as was black treacle. For those commodities one had to provide one's own containers - a bottle for vinegar and a jam jar for black treacle. People used black treacle for cooking. Mother used it, I believe, to make ginger puddings and gingerbread. Salt was sold in blocks and these had to be cut up and crushed before use. Yellow soap for washing clothes and neat *carbolic soap* for scrubbing floors was sold by the bar.

Shopping was a much more leisurely business, even in the towns, than it is today. Chairs were provided for customers and one always sat down while one completed one's purchase. Most housewives would expect to taste cheese before buying or to be offered a biscuit before deciding to buy an unusual brand. All tradesmen would offer to deliver purchases and in fact I never remember my mother ever carrying a shopping basket or a parcel. Even when we went to Tiverton the shopkeeper would invariably carry our purchases out to the horse and trap or, after the war, the car. Standards of honesty were high and one could cheerfully leave parcels in an open trap or car in the sure knowledge that nothing would be taken.

The range of tinned foods available was not large. They were largely confined to fruit such as peaches, apricots and Bartlett pears, and fish such as John West salmon, or Skipper's sardines. Fish and meat pastes were sold in small glass jars. Lyle's golden syrup was sold in similar tins as are used today, as were HP and Worcester sauces. About the only vegetables available out of season were haricot beans and dried peas. These latter had to be soaked in water overnight before cooking.

There were three kinds of matches available - Bryant & May's safety matches - so called because they could only be ignited by striking them on the box, England's Glory and Swann Vestas. One could buy a dozen boxes of Bryant and May's or England's Glory for one penny; Swann Vestas were slightly dearer. Swann also made matches known as Wax Vestas; the stems of these were made of wax instead of wood and were rather smaller than the normal Swann Vestas. Gentlemen often carried these wax vestas in little silver boxes attached to the end of their watch-chain. They could be ignited by rubbing on a corrugated surface on one end of the box.

At Christmas all shopkeepers would give their customers a calendar and if the customer was particularly valued, a present of a box of biscuits or chocolates. Butchers would give valued customers a couple of pounds of sausages or even a small joint of pork. During the war we dealt with a large grocery store in Tiverton which had a wine and spirit licence. They used to send around a man on a bicycle weekly to take orders and the following week the order was delivered by horse-drawn van. From this store we always received a bottle of port and a bottle of sherry at Christmas.

My father went to Tiverton at least once a week where business took him to the bank and often to the County Court (fig. 32). Sometimes in the holidays he would take me with him and take me to a barber's shop for a haircut. In every barber's shop at that time there was a long shelf above the mirrors along which was ranged a row of shaving mugs, each with its own shaving brush. These were the days before the advent of the ubiquitous shaving safety razor - the only type of razor available being the long handled 'cut-throat'.

Many men disliked shaving themselves and preferred to have the job done by a barber. They would usually call in for a shave on their way to work or alternatively on their way home. Most of them would buy their own shaving mugs and brush which the barber would keep for their exclusive use. The cost of a shave was 1d. or 2d. according to the standing of the shop and its clientèle. Boys started work in

Figure 32. Fore Street, Tiverton, showing the Town Hall, where the County Court was held

these shops as soon as they left school and were known as 'lather boys'. In addition to sweeping up the floor and doing odd jobs, they also lathered the customers' faces. At very busy times, usually morning and evening, one lather boy and the barber would look after half a dozen chairs without keeping customers waiting. The lather boy would work along the line of chairs lathering one face after another and, with extraordinary speed, the barber would work his way along after him. Between the rush hours the customer would enjoy a much more leisurely shave which was usually rounded off by having a face massage with some form of lotion. After the massage, the barber would tilt the chair until the customer was almost horizontal and then swathe his face with hot towels for five or ten minutes.

One of the main features of the barber's shop was the rotary hair brush - a shaft fitted with pulley wheels was suspended from the ceiling and a pulley at one end was connected via a rubber belt to a large wheel mounted on one wall at about chest height. After one's hair had been cut the barber would take a cylindrical shaped brush about 6 inches [15cm] in diameter which could rotate freely, on a shaft fitted with a handle at each end. A pulley was attached to the top of the brush and this in turn was connected to a pulley on the overhead shaft by a rubber belt. The lather boy would turn the wheel on the wall like mad and the rotary brush held by the barber would whiz around at quite a high speed. The barber would then proceed to massage one's head all over with the spinning brush. This was supposed to stimulate the roots of the hair. The combination of a very stiff bristled brush and a heavy-handed barber made one feel as if one's scalp was being torn off.

After the rotary brush treatment most men would have their hair singed. This operation was carried out by means of a lighted taper - the barber carefully singeing the ends of the freshly cut hair. The idea of this treatment was that each hair was in fact a tiny tube and unless the ends of these tubes were sealed off all the strength of the hair would drain from the roots. It was generally held that singeing was a specific against premature baldness. To complete the process a little *bay rum* was usually massaged into the scalp and finished by the application of liquid *brilliantine*.

In tobacconists' shops, quite a lot of tobacco was sold loose. Although the well-known national brands were pre-packed, in every tobacconist's one would notice a shelf full of tobacco jars each labelled with a customer's name. Many men preferred to have their tobacco blended to their own individual tastes and these blends were made up by the tobacconist and kept separately in individual jars. My father often sent me into his tobacconist's at Tiverton where I would ask for 'two ounces of Mr Cluett's mixture'. This would be duly weighed out from my father's jar and handed to me without demur.

None of the shops in the village sold fish, but we were not entirely fishless as a man used to cycle out from Tiverton about once a fortnight with a basket of fish mounted on the handlebars. This stock consisted of smoked haddock, kippers, bloaters and a particularly nauseating kind of dried fish. I don't know how this was supposed to be cooked but I imagine that it was first soaked in water and then either boiled or made into a pie. If we wanted fresh fish we had to get this from Tiverton which boasted a very good fish shop. As with all fish shops of this period the window was always open to the street and the fish was displayed on a marble slab. In summer the fish was kept cool with the aid of lumps of ice and two or three times during the day the slab with its display of fish would be hosed down in order to wash the dust off. When available we had smoked haddock at breakfast but fried kippers were always a tea time dish. In addition to the ordinary wet fish we could buy lobsters and crabs from the Tiverton shop and they also sold cockles and winkles. We sometimes had a pint of winkles at tea time. Served with bread and butter, I always found them very tasty although they were not particularly appetising to look at. The trouble with winkles was that of having to remove them from their shells with the aid of a pin - rather a tedious business. One stuck the pin into the blunt end of the winkle and then with a sort of corkscrew motion wriggled it out from its shell. This technique took some little practice to acquire. Mother also used to prepare mackerel by steeping them in spiced vinegar - another tea-time dish. This was known as soused mackerel.

Figure 33. The Post Office, below Sampford Peverell Bridge

Our small post office was on the east side of the canal bridge and was thus situated in Lower Town (fig. 33). The post office was presided over by a rather sweet but very dreamy middle-aged spinster called Miss Taylor. She, poor soul, had the misfortune to fall under the influence of a local man called Bert Cornish. Bert suffered from hip disease and went around the village on crutches[1], doing any little job he could for the odd copper or two. One of his jobs was pumping the church organ and he used to help out at the post office as part-time postman and telegraph boy. Telegrams were delivered on the assumption that they were always harbingers of bad news and that therefore there was never any hurry about delivering them. If one arrived for someone in one of the outlying farms Miss Taylor would wait until the end of school and then get one of the children going in that particular direction to deliver it. Telegrams for anyone in the village proper were delivered by Bert and what with his one good leg and two crutches he was not a notably fast mover. In addition to this he was in the habit of stopping to discuss the contents of the telegram with everyone he happened to meet. Although this made for rather long delivery times, thanks to the astonishing efficiency of the village bush telegraph

---

1. On 18th November, 1915 the Devon & Somerset News reported: "Whilst at a ringing practice at Sampford Peverell Mr Bert Cornish fell and broke his leg. He is progressing favourably" There is no evidence that he suffered from hip disease

it usually happened that the person to whom the telegram was addressed knew all about it before the actual message arrived. On the whole, the village approved this method of delivery since it enabled everyone to keep right up to date with bad news and also it spared the recipient of an unheralded buff-coloured envelope a very nasty shock.

By some means Bert Cornish achieved an extraordinary ascendancy over the postmistress and seemed to enjoy complete freedom to use the post office and its contents as he wished. Came the inevitable day when a couple of inspectors from head office arrived and found that a quantity of stamps and postal orders could not be accounted for. Poor dreamy Miss Taylor was indicted, tried at Exeter assizes and sent down for five years[1]. The general opinion in the village was that Bert Cornish was the real culprit although no proof of this was ever found.

Before 1914 there were no statutory opening and closing times for shops or public houses. On Saturday most shops stayed open to 10pm or later as a matter of course. With the advent of war an Act of Parliament called the Defence of the Realm Act, always referred to as DORA, was passed and, amongst other regulations, limited opening and closing hours (Appendix 7).

---

1. Twelve months – see Appendix 4

Chapter 3

The Village School

Compared to the average village school, I suppose ours at Sampford Peverell had an exceptionally large number of pupils owing to the presence of a large building at the bottom of the village known as St Boniface Home for waifs and strays. This was a charitable institution run by the Church of England and housed about sixty boys between the ages of ten and fourteen who attended the village school. These lads had been literally picked up off the streets of our big cities and taken into care by a Church of England charitable organisation. None of the boys had any known parents. The home was run by a married couple who were the master and matron and they were helped by an assistant matron. The boys were always referred to in the village as 'the home boys' and were marched to and from the school under the supervision of a senior boy (fig. 34). They were all dressed alike in blue jerseys, shorts and long black stockings pulled above the knee and secured by elastic garters. In this respect they were almost indistinguishable from the rest of us who attended school since we all dressed roughly the same (Appendix 2).

Figure 34. St Boniface Home boys returning from school

The school building was divided into three classrooms. One was allocated to the infants and presided over by a mistress. A second was under the charge of another mistress who taught Standard I and the third room, which was the biggest, housed Standards II, III, IV and V. At one end of this large room Standards II and III were taught by an assistant master and at the other end sat Standards IV and V presided over by the headmaster, a Mr Smith. There were no other rooms. If any member of the staff decided to stay on the premises during the lunchtime break, they had to eat their sandwiches in their classroom since no room was available for them to use as a staff room.

Figure 35. 'Marble arch', with school entrance on left

All toilets were outside, remote from the school building (fig. 35) at the end of a long playground and the only washing facilities were a couple of washbasins in the porch at the rear entrance. These were supplied with cold water taps. No school meals were provided and the children who lived in outlying districts usually brought along some sandwiches or a crust of bread and cheese and a piece of cake for their lunch. Cold water from the washbasin taps was available for a drink. Quite a few of the children had to walk a couple of miles each way to and from the school. This, I suppose, was not unpleasant in good weather, but must have been uncomfortable in winter since there were no facilities for drying clothes. When we lived at Boobery I had to walk about half a mile each way and although I was always well wrapped up and furnished with a sou'wester hat in wet weather, it was not unusual to sit through a morning or afternoon with sodden boots and stockings. However, no-one seemed to bother overmuch about little things like that and, in fact, all the children seemed to thrive on it. I never remember one epidemic of any sort in the village all the time I was at school.

EPIDEMICS
Extracts from School Log Book
March 8th 1912
Attendance continues poor owing to the prevalence of mumps.
28th March 1913
School reassembled with a very poor attendance. Cases of illness among the boys from St Boniface Home had been found to be scarlet fever. Consequently the whole of the "Home" boys will be absent from school for some weeks. The attendance was as follows: Number on Books 128   Number present   65
February 28th 1918
Attendance is poor among the younger children owing to the prevalence of Whooping cough

Children were seldom kept away on account of illness although remedies available were of the simplest. For instance, the only medicines my mother kept in the house were syrup of figs, Venos Lightning cough cure and Fennings fever cure. For cuts and abrasions the standard treatment was the application of iodine or boracic ointment. The ointment was always sold in small round fibre boxes and since I, in common with most of the other children, had perpetual scabby knees or skinned shins through climbing trees or falling down on the stone roads, mother always kept in a good stock of ointment. When we had bad colds, which often caused wheezy chests, our chests were rubbed with *camphorated oil* before bed. Not infrequently we suffered from swollen glands in the neck. For this complaint the standard treatment was to sleep with a woollen stocking tied around the neck. The usual treatment for sore throats was a dose of honey mixed with vinegar. These remedies just about covered all the illnesses to which we were prey. We had a doctor resident in the village but as he was seldom called in except for births, deaths and broken limbs, he was not a great deal better off than most of his patients. Our Dr MacDonald was a great friend of my father's and in later years Dad took a great delight in telling me how he would often help MacDonald dispense medicines. These consisted mostly of pump water with different colouring and flavouring agents mixed in. I don't suppose MacDonald had ever heard of psychology but he certainly knew the value of faith since his patients used to swear by his medicines.

I suppose it must have been soon after my fifth birthday that I first went to school and entered the infants' class. Here we immediately started to learn our numbers and simple addition and subtraction with the aid of an abacus (fig. 36) which, as I recall, was the only piece of apparatus in the school. I remember so clearly the mistress flicking the beads of the abacus along the wires as we chanted:

One, two, three, four, five,
Catching fishes all alive.
Six, seven, eight, nine, ten,
Then we let them go again.

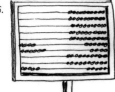

Figure 36.

We learned to read by chanting the alphabet and with the use of small, limp cloth-covered reading books. These contained short sentences such as 'the cat sat on the mat', 'the big cat saw the rat', and 'the cat ran after the rat'. All the two syllable words were hyphenated.

There was no general assembly in the mornings but each teacher would read a passage from the Bible to the class and we followed this by chanting the Lord's prayer. I don't think that any of us had any idea what this prayer was about since the words we all chanted were 'Are for chart Nevan'. It was a considerable time before it dawned upon me that these cryptic words meant 'Our Father which art in Heaven'.

Before we left the infants' class we were all expected to be capable of reading simple English and to have a working knowledge of simple addition and subtraction. As soon as the master or mistress concerned decided that one was capable of advancement one was moved up into a higher class. There were never any examinations. I remember I went up into Standard I after a couple of terms in the infants', by which time I was already able to read fairy stories and children's books. I was probably luckier than most of the children in this respect since our home was always full of books, papers and magazines. Reading was almost second nature to me.

Our first job in Standard I was to learn our tables. We did this by chanting them over and over again until we knew them forwards, backwards and sideways. We then started on simple multiplication and division and, of course, writing. At this stage all our sums and writing were done on slates (fig. 37). Even today I have only to recall the squeak of the slate pencils as they moved over the slates for my teeth to be set on edge. In due course we were issued with copy books and for writing in these we were provided

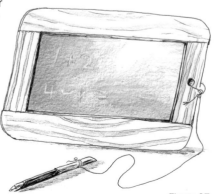

Figure 37.

with pencils. These copy books had highly moral maxims, usually proverbs, printed in copperplate script at the top of each page, and we spent a great part of our time trying to reproduce this. Actually, this type of practice writing was carried on through the school right up to Standard V.

Most of our time was spent on reading, writing, and arithmetic with the occasional lesson on scripture, geography and history. One afternoon each week the girls practised sewing and the boys did drawing. Most lessons were given verbally by the teachers with the aid of blackboard and chalk, since there were no books other than the standard reading books.

At many village schools of this era the boys were taught gardening during the girls' sewing afternoon. This usually meant that the boys dug and looked after the headmaster's garden as the school house usually adjoined the school. At Sampford, however, this did not happen as the school house was some little distance from the school and had only a very small garden.

When we graduated to Standard II, which shared the large schoolroom with all the higher classes, we came under the rather cold eye of Mr Moist[1], the assistant master, and it was here that we were introduced to pen and ink. This class was furnished with double desks and here we sat two by two wrestling with blots, crossed nibs and the splutter of ink all over our beautiful copy books. Each desk was furnished with two inkwells (fig. 38) and we were given wooden penholders with steel nibs. In this class we started to delve into the mysteries of long division and multiplication and spent more and more time learning more and more tables, *avoirdupois*, dry measure, liquid measure etc.

Figure 38.

Discipline was firm but only the Head and the assistant master used the cane. The recipient of such punishment was called to the front of the class, told to hold out his hands and he would then receive a sharp blow with the cane across the palm of each hand in turn. This was more than a little painful. This treatment not only reinforced discipline but reminded us to focus our energies more fully on the lesson, rather than on kicking our neighbours' shins under the desk.

1. Sidney Charles Moyse – joined the school staff February 1914

Although boys and girls often sat together in class, the sexes were segregated into different playgrounds at playtime, the girls being separated from the boys by a high wall. This was just as well since there was no playtime supervision by the staff and we boys used to play some pretty rough games; so much so that cuts and bruises were so common as to be completely ignored. In fact, I don't think that there was even a primitive first-aid box in the school. If we acquired a badly cut knee with a fair amount of blood involved, the standard treatment was to bind it up with our handkerchiefs. Handkerchiefs tended to be rather despised, most of the children preferring to wipe their noses on their jersey sleeves, and most jersey sleeves soon acquired a shiny patina which looked as if snails had been crawling over them.

The school bell was mounted on the roof of the building and this was rung every morning at a quarter to nine. It was rung again at nine o'clock by which time we were all expected to be sitting in our places with our faces moulded into expressions of expectant eagerness, preparatory to starting the first lesson. Hours of work were the same for all classes including the infants. We would work from nine o'clock until ten thirty when we had a fifteen minute break. We then returned to our classrooms and worked until twelve thirty, when those of us who lived near enough went home for lunch. After lunch we started work at two o' clock and, with a fifteen minute break at three, we carried on until school ended at four o'clock.

During the last period on Friday afternoons the four classes in the large schoolroom joined in singing. We had a standard songbook which, I imagine, was issued to all schools at that time. Thus we learned such songs as 'Who Will O'er the Downs With Me?' (Appendix 3), 'Hearts of Oak', 'Men of Harlech' and 'God Bless the Prince of Wales'. On one or two occasions we were visited by itinerant entertainers, one of whom, I remember, recited monologues of great dramatic content about dying *paupers*, and once we had a visit from a conjurer who produced chocolate drops from a bowler hat. This just about covered our contact with the dramatic arts.

When we eventually gained the two top standards, IV and V, we found that the emphasis was still concentrated upon reading, writing and arithmetic. Here, under the eye of the headmaster we learned to write essays and précis pieces of prose. We were also taught the mysteries of percentages and were given problems about trying to fill a bath with water when somebody had left the plug out. I am convinced that the mental blockage I have always experienced about arithmetic occurred here, not only because it seemed such a stupid thing to do but also because I, like everyone else in the village, had never heard of a plumbed-in bath, let alone one which had a plug in the bottom.

Figure 39.

After prayers in the morning the first period was always arithmetic, when the headmaster would set us some sums to do. While we were struggling with these the Head would sit on a high stool at his desk (fig. 39) and read the Daily Mail. At this time the Daily Mail always printed in it a humorous column on the leader page, and sometimes when the Head found this article particularly amusing he would call for the attention of the class by striking a bell on his desk, and would read the article aloud to us. Unfortunately, after reading the first two or three sentences, he usually became quite incoherent with laughter, tears would roll down his cheeks and the more he read the less we understood. Nevertheless, we all felt duty bound to roll around with laughter and some of the more exuberant spirits would deliberately fall off their forms in ecstasies of simulated mirth.

At the bottom of the village was a large playing field owned by the St Boniface Home Authorities and in one corner of this was an open-air swimming pool. On fine summer afternoons, after school hours, the Headmaster would take a party of us along to this pool and give us some swimming lessons.

THE SWIMMING POOL

Sampford Peverell's swimming pool was situated in the grounds of Buckland Cottage, which is adjacent to Buckland Bridge, and was supplied with water from the canal. The structure was probably built in 1814, at the same time as the canal, and its original purpose is believed to have been a tannery tank for soaking hides. A few yards along the towpath to the east of Buckland Bridge, the top of an archway can still be seen today. It was under this archway that the channel supplying water to the swimming pool used to pass.

Extract from the School Log Book 14th June 1912
Visits to the Swimming Bath have been resumed, but without encroaching materially on the school time. The Master takes such of the village boys as desire to avail themselves of the opportunity at once after afternoon school prayers, prayers being taken a little earlier than 4.15 when possible. The "St Boniface Home" boys are taken by their own staff at 5 pm. It was found that taking the upper standard boys in school time interfered too much with the last lessons.

Once a year the school was visited by an inspector. We always knew when this official was coming since for about a week before the great day the teachers tended to become very edgy. On the eve of the visit we were always enjoined, under threat of dire penalties, to turn up at school the next morning with clean hands, faces and shining boots. On arrival at the school the inspector would visit each class in turn and start firing questions at the children while the teacher hovered nervously in the background, surreptitiously wiping clammy palms, as they knew that their efficiency as teachers would be judged by the performance of the class. I think they must have suffered agonies as the inspector would unerringly pick out the biggest dunderheads in the class to answer the most difficult questions. We all heaved sighs of relief when we saw the last of him.

SCHOOL INSPECTIONS
Extract from School Log Book
1st September 1914
The Report of the Diocesan Inspector is as follows:
"The Headmaster and his staff deserve congratulations for the condition of the school. There is a fine tone in all the groups. Combined with rare enthusiasm there is good intelligence. The older children have been taught to "think" and they appreciate fully much of the applicative side of both the Scripture History and the Catechism. The opening of school was delightful. The school is classed as "Excellent".
Honourable Mention: Denis Snow .....Reginald Russell....... D. Cluett ...... C. Jefferys (43 names in all)

From time to time we were visited by a woman who used to examine the children's heads for fleas and once we had a visit from a dentist. I remember he decided that I needed two teeth filling and he carried out this operation in the playground with the aid of a foot-drill. However, both fillings fell out a couple of days later and eventually both hollow teeth broke off. This experience completely cured me of any desire to have teeth filled in the future and, in fact, I never did .

SCHOOL HEALTH CHECKS
Extracts from School Log Book
4th April 1916 Dental examination. The majority of the parents concerned objected to "treatment"
19th July 1917 Visit of School Dentist. To make the Infants' Room available, the Infants' registers were marked at 9 o'clock, and those infants not wanted by the dentist were sent home at 10.50.
2nd November 1917 School Nurse examined the girls (36 in number) for pediculosis.
10th December 1917
The school re-examined 12 girls for pediculosis, - but was able to report great improvement.

pediculosis =lousiness

Chapter 4

The Church

When we came to Sampford Peverell in 1909 the Rector was the Rev. Philip Rossiter, nephew of George William Rossiter Ireland who had died the previous year after more than 50 years as Rector. However, Philip Rossiter had the living for only 2 years before he, too, died and for the rest of the time that I lived in the village the incumbent was J.J. Rees (fig. 40).

Rees was a typical small dark Welshman and, as far as I can remember, he and his family took no part at all in the life of the village. In fact, apart from attending church services, his wife and two daughters were never seen. Mrs Rees had the appearance of a rather bedraggled gypsy woman, but we only caught glimpses of her as she scuttled like a frightened mouse across the road to and from the services. Neither of the children, as far as I know, ever went to school.

Figure 40. Rev. John James Rees, circa 1938

From time to time one would encounter Rees in the village. Sometimes he would speak to people but more often he would ignore everyone. On these occasions he would walk along the street with his eyes on the ground looking, as it was often said, as if he had the Devil in him. For all his faults, however, I think he was fond of the village children. He certainly seemed more at home with us than he did with the adults. I remember he would often join a group of kids in a game of marbles in the roadway.

A year or two after we arrived at Sampford he distinguished himself by turning up drunk to officiate at a funeral and it was only by the combined efforts of the mourners that he was saved from falling into the grave on top of the coffin. This episode seemed to steady him up for a time and he did not appear drunk in public until some years later one Sunday evening when he was drunk at evensong. It happened that on this particular evening my mother was the organist. When she started the *voluntary* at the beginning of the service it was at once apparent that something was wrong with the parson. He wove his way very uncertainly up the aisle to the reading desk and on arriving there kept repeating 'Dearly beloved brethren' over and over again. Eventually he did manage to get the service started but what with reading the prayers and responses in all the wrong places the whole thing became rather a shambles. In addition to this, when the time came for the first hymn, he gave out the wrong hymn number which resulted in Mother playing one hymn while the congregation was singing another. However, he managed to scramble through the service until the moment arrived for the sermon. With great difficulty he managed to climb into the pulpit. Arriving there he stood for several moments completely speechless and then, without the slightest warning, disappeared from view as his legs gave way and he slid gently down the pulpit steps to the floor of the chancel. Two of the churchwardens came forward and, lifting him up, began to proceed slowly down the aisle, one on each side of him, while Mother, at the organ, valiantly extemporised variations on the last hymn 'Lead Kindly Light'.

Figure 41. St. John the Baptist Church

The mainstay of the Parish church (fig. 41) and the power behind the scenes was Emma Dunn. Emma was a little woman, all of 4ft. lOin. [148 cms] in her shoes. She was the spinster sister of Cocky Dunn, the Cobbler, and lived in a little cottage a few hundred yards from the church. She had no teeth and her jaws were continually working as if she were perpetually chewing gum. I believe her official job was that of church cleaner but over the years she had managed to establish herself as a sort of general manager. She did everything from ringing the *'Passing Bell'* to decorating the altar. The church was entirely lit by candles. I suppose there must have been a hundred of them altogether and it was Emma who lit them all before the service and extinguished them after the congregation had left.

Emma ruled the congregation with a discipline worthy of any sergeant major and it was she who decided where everyone should sit. It was a most impressive sight to see Emma meet each family at the church door and lead them in procession up the aisle to the appointed pew, where she would usher them one by one into their seats. For some reason best known to herself she had placed our family third row from the front in the centre block. The front of this pew, I remember, was graced by a wrought iron candelabra (fig. 42) carrying three candles. In time we came to refer to this as 'our' pew, since no-one else was allowed to occupy it.

The annual harvest festival service always filled the church to capacity and it was on these occasions that Emma showed her true mettle. Five or ten minutes before the service was due to begin people would start to arrive in force and it was impossible for Emma to escort everyone to the pews, with the result that quite a lot of people would choose their own seats. Emma had no mercy on these interlopers. She would dash around at top speed ordering them out of the seats of their choice

Figure 42.

and pushing them into the pews which best suited her ideas. It always struck me that, when seating people, she had her own system of grading based on the footwear of the congregation, since anyone turning up with hobnail boots was firmly shooed to the back rows. Not infrequently the service would be held up for five or ten minutes until she had sorted everyone out to her own satisfaction.

During services Emma always sat at the back of the church from where she could survey the congregation with an eagle eye and woe betide any child who was unduly restless or made too much noise by scuffing his hobnail boots along the front of the pew. On such occasions Emma would be out of her seat like a flash and would fetch the offender a clout on the side of the head, which would leave the child in a complete daze for the rest of the service.

The organ, most unusually, was at the rear of the building, and stretched along the west wall for about two thirds of the width of the church. The console was at the north end whilst at the other end, just inside the church door, was a small cubbyhole in which sat the man who blew the organ bellows. The organist could communicate with the organ blower by pulling a little lever and this, via a wire, activated a sort of plumb bob at the blower's end which warned him that the organist wished him to start pumping. The blower was also furnished with a gauge, duplicated at the console, which gave an indication of the amount of air in the bellows.

The regular organist was Mr Smith, the school headmaster, but when he was ill or away on holiday, Mother would deputise for him. The official organ blower was Bert Cornish, the cripple who used to go around the village on crutches. When Mother played the organ I often used to sit with her and one evening service I remember very clearly. The parson reached the end of the sermon and Mother signalled Bert to start pumping. Nothing happened. Again and again she frantically signalled but got no response from Bert. The vicar gave out the number of the hymn and the congregation stood waiting for the organist to start to play. Suddenly in the dead silence a terrific snore echoed through the church. Bert Cornish was asleep. Emma Dunn grasped the situation in a flash and, dashing across the church, seized Bert by the hair and began thumping his head against the back of his wooden seat. Poor old Bert, suddenly galvanised into action by this treatment, automatically began to pump like a madman and didn't even stop while the vicar was giving his blessing at the end of the service.

I have already mentioned that when a death occurred in the village it was Emma who rang the 'Passing Bell' or, as we called it, the 'Death Bell'. When the deceased was a man, this was rung once a minute for an hour. For a woman it was rung for half an hour. As far as the bells were concerned, however, the carillon was her especial pride and joy (fig. 43). This allowed an operator to play tunes on the bells, and Emma would play it whenever the fancy took her irrespective of the time of day or what was going on in the village. Unfortunately she only knew two tunes: 'Now the day is over' and 'Highland Laddie'. Thus it was no uncommon experience to be awakened at 6.00 am on a bright summer's morning by the strains of 'Now the day is over' pealing out from the church tower, or to watch the slow procession of a funeral cortège to the accompaniment of Emma's version of 'Highland Laddie'.

> **CARILLON**
> The carillon at Sampford Peverell Church was a mechanism which enabled one person to play simple tunes on the church bells. This consisted of six pivoted hammers attached to the bell frame, each one adjacent to a different bell. A cord from each hammer was fed down, via pulleys, to the ground floor of the bell chamber, where they were gathered in one corner. The carillon fell into disuse in about 1950.

Sampford Peverell did not boast a hearse, so all funeral processions were on foot led by the coffin on a bier. The bier was basically a couple of planks mounted on four wheels and the pall bearers, three on each side, pushed it to the church. Most people, except the very poorest, had a suit of black and women had a black dress for these occasions and, if the deceased was a married man, his widow would be dressed in black from head to foot with a heavy black veil over her face. She usually wore this outfit for several months after the funeral whenever she appeared in public. A man who had been bereaved by the loss of a near relative usually wore

CARILLON ASSEMBLY AND ACTION

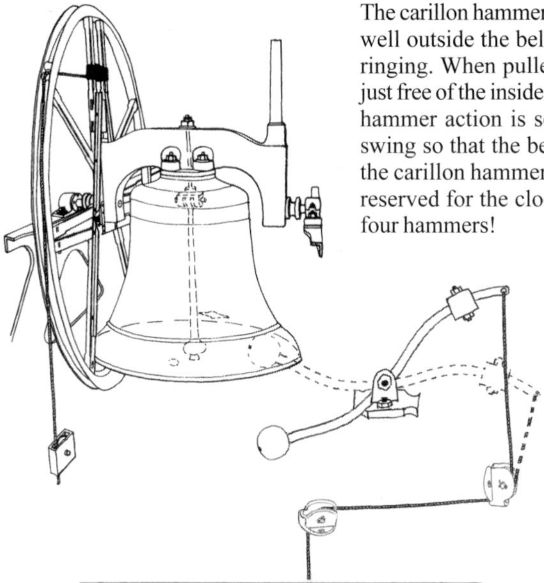

The carillon hammers are here shown at rest, positioned well outside the bell revolution action during normal ringing. When pulled up the carillon hammer is held just free of the inside of the bell rim surface. The carillon hammer action is set up at right angles to the bell's swing so that the bell does not move when struck by the carillon hammer. The outside surface of the bell is reserved for the clock strike hammers, another set of four hammers!

The hammers are pulled up to the rim by ropes each re-directed by a series of pulleys and which are finally assembled and spaced by a block of pulleys above the ringing mechanism, so that they line up with the block of rollers below the hymn sheet.

This is an actual set of hymn instructions as used at Sampford Peverell. The operator has to decide the rhythm required by the tune.

This is the area where the ropes are pulled to ring the bells to make the tune, toll for a funeral or ring a simple peal.

The rod in the centre of the roller is used to turn the roller to take up the slack in the ropes and raise the hammers to their pre-determined positions ready for ringing. The tension on the ropes is maintained by a ratchet mechanism on the right of the roller.

Figure 43.

50

an armband of black crêpe or even a diamond shaped piece of black material sewn on to the sleeve of his jacket. During a period of mourning the immediate family would usually use black-edged note-paper for their letters and post them in black-edged envelopes.

VILLAGE STOCKS
Up to about 1850, stocks were used to punish people for committing offences, such as being drunk, swearing, or being a 'vagabond' (homeless person). Although most stocks were destroyed, Sampford Peverell's were preserved by the Rector and are now a museum piece.

The churchyard extended around three sides of the church. The fourth side, on the north, was unconsecrated ground and it was here that suicides and unbaptised children were buried without the benefit of a funeral service. Unbaptised children were buried here by the father after dark. The village stocks stood against the north side of the church but I never met anyone who could remember them having been used (fig. 44).

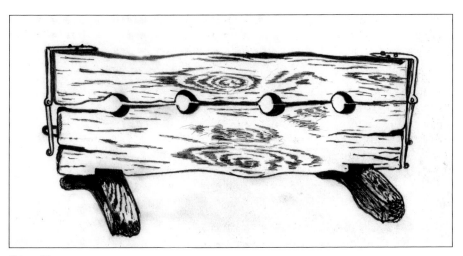

Figure 44.

Paupers were buried in a communal grave which could be reopened at any time for the purpose of adding another coffin. The funeral expenses in these cases were paid for by the parish and people considered it a terrible disgrace if one of the family was ever buried 'on the Parish'. Even the poorest people would save a penny or halfpenny a week almost all their lives so that they could be buried 'decently'. There was no undertaker in the village; the coffin would be made by the local carpenter[1].

1. Probably Charles Hussey at Moor End

Many people at this time had a great fear of being buried alive and it was not uncommon for instructions to be left requesting a doctor to open an artery before interment. I suspect that this fear was not altogether without foundation, since doctors were quite rough and ready in their diagnoses and would pronounce any person to be dead if they could not feel a heartbeat. Mother often told a story which gave some point to this feeling. It appears that when she was a young girl living at her home in Langport, a man died and the death certificate was duly signed. The man's wife, however, firmly refused to accept that he was dead, since she claimed that he had not lost his colour. No-one took any notice of her, so early in the morning on the day of the funeral she set off to consult the local 'wise woman' who lived just outside the village. This old woman gave the wife the following advice. 'Go home and heat a silver florin in the fire until it is too hot to touch. Then, take the hot coin and lay it on the bare breast of the alleged corpse. If the skin blisters then the man is alive.' The wife went home and carried out the test and Mother used to describe vividly how she remembered the woman rushing down the village street screaming out at the top of her voice, 'My God 'ees blistered, My God 'ees blistered!' However, blisters or no blisters they buried him the same afternoon.

Sampford also boasted a small Wesleyan chapel (fig. 45). There was no resident chapel minister in the parish so I suppose they had to rely on lay preachers. For some reason chapel people were rather looked down upon in our predominantly church-going community and they were referred to as 'chapel-dodgers'. It was always assumed that, by defin-ition, they were hypocrites. Strangely this religious line which divided the villagers

Figure 45. Wesleyan Methodist Chapel in Higher Town

also divided them politically, since 'chapel dodgers' were always thought to be Liberals.

At this time Socialism had not been heard of in the village and when, towards the end of the war, rumours of this strange political mutation began to seep through, it was looked upon as some form of disease to be found only in towns 'up country'. During the last few months of the war however, my father engaged a woman clerk who lived in Tiverton and commuted to and from work on a bicycle. It transpired that she was an ardent socialist and had even addressed meetings on the subject. The village was not unduly agitated by the advent of this phenomenon and always treated her with the amused but kindly tolerance usually accorded to the mentally handicapped.

Chapter 5

Christmas

The highlight of the year for all the children was, of course, Christmas, and its harbinger was, for me, about the end of October when Mother made the Christmas puddings. These were mixed in a great earthenware pan into which were thrown quantities of chopped fruit and *suet*, liberally moistened with dark draught beer. In addition to the puddings required for the Christmas period, sufficient of the mixture was made to provide a pudding for each of our several birthdays throughout the year. When the pudding was mixed it was considered obligatory for everyone who happened to be in the house at the time to have a stir. When it was ready it was transferred to basins which were then tied up in white cloths and put in the steamer to cook. After cooking they were transferred to a cool *pantry* where they would keep for as long as required.

It seemed an endless time from October to Christmas, especially as none of the adults seemed to evince the slightest interest in the event. About ten days before Christmas, however, signs of the festival began to appear as the village shop windows were, one by one, decorated with tinsel, paper bells, sugar mice, and possibly a few oranges and nuts for good measure. We were all completely entranced by these marvellous decorations, and a few days before Christmas Day even the two butchers would enter into the spirit of the season by arranging a pig's head with an orange in its mouth in the centre of their respective windows.

As the days were ticked off the calendar, so the pace quickened. At home my first real excitement was tasted when the Christmas numbers of periodicals arrived. At this time we took three weeklies - Titbits, Answers and Pearson's Weekly. Unlike their descendants today, these were real family papers and the Christmas numbers were about double their normal size and packed with ghost stories, puzzles, jokes and games to play at parties. I used to love these papers and when the special numbers appeared I knew that the Christmas season had really begun. By the beginning of the final week things really began to get hectic. Mother and Father would be immersed in masses of brown paper and cardboard boxes as they packed parcels to send off to all the relatives and friends, while every day the postman would arrive at the door with parcels for us. Then the cooking would start and this would go on almost continuously until Christmas Eve when the last batch of mince pies was taken from the oven. Mother always cooked a ham, an ox tongue and a large pork pie in addition to all the cakes, tarts etc. The Christmas cake was always cooked and iced some little time before Christmas. The last culinary job to be done on Christmas Eve was the final preparations to make the turkey ready for the oven next morning.

Every year on the day before Christmas Eve my uncle and aunt and their boy - about the same age as my brother, Ray - would come to stay with us and, while my aunt helped Mother on Christmas Eve, the rest of us decorated the house. On the afternoon of Christmas Eve it was always my job to go out and get the holly for the decorations, which I did in the company of my friend Reg Russell, and in the waning light of the December afternoon I would arrive home with masses of holly and covered in scratches from head to foot.

On Christmas morning I always awoke at some unearthly hour and lit the candle beside my bed in order to take a quick look at my presents. These were never very expensive and usually consisted of things like a mouth organ, tin whistle - I could play tunes on these from as far back as I can remember - perhaps a pocket knife and a board game of some sort. In addition I used to get two or three books which pleased me most of all. After having seen my presents I would put out the light and wait for seven o'clock.

At seven in the morning the church bells would begin to ring and this was the signal for me to take my presents to my parents' room for their inspection. We always had breakfast fairly early since not only had the preparations for the Christmas dinner to go forward but all sorts of people used to drop in for a drink and a mince pie from about 10.30 onwards. By 11 o'clock there seemed to be a continuous stream of people coming and going.

The callers were usually headed by the village policeman who seemed always to be the first to arrive and the last to depart. Bobby Blackmore, as we children knew him, was a huge man with a heavy black moustache and a great rounded belly which was only saved from bursting by his thick black leather uniform belt. He had never been known to make an arrest[1]. His idea of justice was simple but firm. Any transgressor, whether man or child, was given a good thrashing on the spot and sent home. There was seldom any trouble when Bobby Blackmore was on his beat. He used to make a point of knocking on our door when he was making his night rounds and Father would ask him in for a drink. During the

Figure 46.

1. See Appendix 5

hours of darkness he always carried an oil-burning bull's eye lantern clipped on to his belt (fig. 46). This had a shutter which could be turned across the bull's eye to cut off the light when required

When we had finally got rid of all the callers, final preparations were made for dinner and we usually sat down to this at about 1 pm. This always followed the traditional pattern of turkey, sprouts etc. with chestnut sauce and redcurrant jelly. This was followed by Christmas pudding and mince pies. I remember one memorable year however when we did not get the pudding. Mother went to the kitchen for it and, after decorating it with a sprig of holly and igniting the brandy which had been poured over it, she proceeded to bring it to the dining-room door. However, she stumbled and the pudding shot straight off the dish and caught Father full in the back of the neck. Father sprang high in the air using several expressions which could not be interpreted as tidings of comfort and joy. We, in turn, leaped from our chairs and rushed to remove the bits of flaming pudding which had distributed itself fairly evenly over his person. Calm was eventually restored but we had no sooner sat down again when we were disturbed by a most peculiar noise coming from a corner of the room. Our eyes turned to the direction of the noise and there, in an armchair, was our old cat triumphantly giving birth to the last of five kittens. This seemed to be the last straw as far as Father was concerned. He rose to his feet, addressed a few pithy remarks to the assembled company on the subject of the hazards of life in a lunatic asylum and, pausing only to remove the holly sprig which had been lodged between his collar and the back of his neck, made a beeline for the kitchen and the bottle of brandy.

Chapter 6

A Visit to Grannie's

If the traveller leaves the little North Devon village of Chittlehampton and follows the lane towards the village of Chittlehamholt, he will arrive, after about one and a half miles, at a farmhouse on the right hand side of the road. Directly opposite, across the lane, are two small whitewashed thatched cottages. This small cluster

Figure 47. Grannie and Granfer's cottage at Ambow, as it is today

of buildings is called Ambow, and in the second of the two cottages (fig. 47) lived my great-grandfather and his wife: Henry and Elizabeth Simmons.

Ambow today is exactly the same as I first saw it in 1912, at the welcome end of the long two and a half mile uphill walk from Umberleigh railway station. I was four and a half and had been carried most of the way on my father's back. We turned in at the small white wicket gate, walked up the path, and I was set down before the stone porch and then helped up two steep stone steps to the open front door where Granfer Simmons and Grannie were waiting to welcome us.

My memories of them are vague. At that time Granfer Simmons had passed his one hundredth birthday and Grannie was a year or two younger[1]. The flickering pictures crossing my mind reveal a tall, rather gaunt, woman, wearing a large white apron and leaning on a stick. Of my great-grandfather's appearance I can remember nothing.

They had lived all their married lives in the cottage, which at the time was about two hundred years old. The Simmons family had been connected with Ambow for several hundred years. One of my uncles discovered, at Bideford, records referring to the Admiral of Bideford who had been instructed by Queen Elizabeth I to fit out warships a year or two before the Armada. The records show a contract placed with one Henry Simmons of Chittlehampton, a smith by trade, to make iron hoops for the ships' gunpowder barrels, so I suppose the family could claim to have rendered some assistance in repelling the Armada. That the Henry Simmons referred to was a forbear is probably true, since we do know that at one time there was a smithy situated behind the cottage.

My great-grandfather worked on the land all his life. As a very young man he led a team of freelance reapers: when harvest time was approaching, these young men would walk from Chittlehampton to Bridgwater with their scythes over their shoulders and their long sharpening stones thrust through loops in their leather belts. They would make contracts with farmers to carry out the reaping, working each field as a team. They worked from dawn to dusk and slept in the farm barns at night. Their contracts with the farmers usually included food and cider. The reaping season over, they would sling their scythes across their shoulders and tramp the forty or fifty miles home again.

The main landowner in the Chittlehampton area was Lord Clinton and Granfer eventually got a job on his estate. In due course he became chief forester and

1. The family gravestone in Chittlehampton churchyard includes the deaths of Henry Simmons: 16th January 1915, aged 87 and Elizabeth Simmons 31st January 1917, aged 90

held this job until he retired. He was responsible for planting most of the trees and woods in the area, and to this day an avenue of trees planted by him (fig. 48) still shades the path from the lychgate to the west door of Chittlehampton Church.

There were about one and a half acres of land belonging to the cottage at Ambow and also a big apple orchard. I remember when a big cherry tree grew just inside the garden wall opposite the front door. A bell had been rigged in this tree and I spent many hours during the cherry season as a child pulling on a length of rope and ringing the bell to scare the birds away. In later years this tree was felled.

Grannie and Granfer kept pigs and poultry and also used some of the land as a market garden. They also owned a donkey and cart. Every week the cart would be loaded with garden produce: fruit,

Figure 48. The avenue of trees at Chittlehampton Church, as it is today

poultry and eggs – and off Grannie would go to South Molton market five miles away. She would sit in the market on a stool surrounded by the produce until it was all sold. She always walked to and from the market, leading the donkey, which they thought so much of that no-one was ever allowed to ride on the cart in case it tired the beast.

Granfer Simmons had never been to school but had taught himself to read and write. I remember, when I was older, seeing a couple of very old books on the subject of forest management in which he had written marginal annotations in beautiful copperplate handwriting. I have also been told that he could look at a tree-trunk and judge the amount of useful wood in it to a couple of cubic feet. Apart from the two books I have mentioned, the only other reading matter I can remember seeing in the cottage was the family Bible, which was a huge tome with brass clasps, kept on a side table, flanked by a pair of china dogs. They would have had very little time for reading, since they worked almost all the daylight hours, summer and winter. Of course, apart from tending the pigs and poultry, they never worked on Sundays.

My father often told the story of his first visit to Ambow. Mother was staying there before they were married and he cycled there from Stalbridge, his home in Dorset. Granfer had never in his life seen a bicycle and could not believe it was possible to balance on two wheels. After my father had given him a demonstration, the old man gave it as his profound opinion that the invention had been inspired by the Devil and that no good would come of it.

Notwithstanding this shaky start, however, Dad seems to have become very popular with the old man, as he realised the first time he had Sunday dinner with them. No matter what the rest of the family were having for their meal, it was Granfer's custom to have a shoulder of mutton placed before him. This was his own personal joint and no-one else was allowed to touch it. It was considered a mark of great esteem if Granfer offered any visitor a slice from this joint, so Dad felt very honoured when the old man cut off a slice of mutton and put it on his plate. It is interesting to remember that in those days lambs were seldom, if ever, slaughtered for food. One could only buy mutton chops and it was not until the late 1920s that such things as lamb chops came on the market.

Granfer died about a year after my first visit. After his death my grandmother, who was now a widow herself, took over Ambow in order to look after great-grandmother. However, Grannie Simmons had a fall about a year later and died shortly afterwards. Grannie Sowden, my mother's mother, continued to live there for many years and I was often sent there for holidays during the years of the First World War. As Ambow never changed, I was able to have first-hand experience of how Grannie and Granfer had lived for the best part of one hundred years.

The cottage was built of cob and thatched. Cob is a mixture of clay, farmyard dung and straw mixed together and rammed hard. As cob is porous, the walls were protected as much as possible by the very deep overhanging thatched eaves. Around the bottom of the walls a two foot band of tar was applied. The walls were whitewashed, or I should say limewashed - a wash made of lime and water. These walls were between two feet and two feet six inches thick. The thick walls, together with the thatched roof and small latticed windows, made the cottage cool in summer and snug and warm in winter.

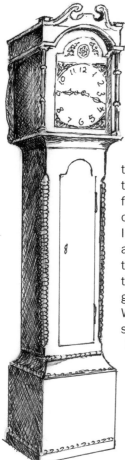

The kitchen, with its stone flagged floor, was also the living room. One stepped directly into the kitchen from the front door and found on one's left a large dresser shelved with plates and meat dishes and hung with cups and saucers. Beyond the dresser stood the grandfather clock. (fig. 49) It was on this clock that I learned to tell the time.

Directly opposite was the fireplace with an open hearth. This consisted of a large recess about five feet high, five feet wide and about three feet from the front to the rear of the hearth, which was of brick and at floor level. Wood was the only fuel used. The fire was usually made towards the front of the hearth and it was possible to step under the lintel of the fireplace and walk right round the fire. As a small boy I spent many dark autumn evenings sitting behind the fire on a three-legged milking stool, listening to my grandmother telling ghost stories and blowing up the smouldering logs with the bellows until they spurted into flame and lit up my grandmother's face as she sat in Granfer's high-backed Windsor chair in front of the fire. (fig.50) The chimney went straight up over the centre of the fireplace, and as one sat behind the fire one could look up and see the stars. Sometimes Grandmother was disinclined to talk and then the only sound in the cottage was the slow tick-tock of the grandfather clock and sometimes the chirping of a cricket on the hearth.

Across the base of the chimney, cemented into the bricks, was a strong iron bar, and hanging

Figure 49.

from this were two lengths of flat iron, each of which had deep teeth cut into one edge. Each of these flat bars supported another flat bar which could be raised or lowered and secured at any height from the fire by engaging a hook in the teeth of the upper bars. The lower ends of the adjustable bars were hooked to the handles of either a three-legged iron crock or a huge iron kettle. These vessels were the only source of hot water and were always filled and kept hanging over the fire. The crock was usually used for cooking stews. Also used on the fire was a trivet.

Figure 50.

(fig. 51) This was a flat iron ring supported by three legs which could be stood in the fire and used as a platform if one wished to use an ordinary iron saucepan or a frying pan. Grannie also had a smaller iron kettle which she used for making tea.

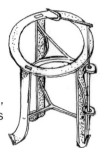

Figure 51.

Built into an outside wall of the fireplace was a large brick oven, furnished with an iron door. The oven was very deep and was built right through the wall, appearing as a large bulge on the outside. It was heated by the simple method of shovelling a layer of hot wood ash all over the oven floor and then filling it with brushwood. The door was left open until all the brushwood was burned and then closed to allow the hot ash to heat the oven. This process might have to be repeated several times before the oven reached the desired heat. When hot enough, all the wood ash was brushed out and bread, pies, cakes etc. were put in and cooked as the oven cooled. Bread cooked by this method was delicious. Grannie often used to make a miniature cottage loaf for me and I used to eat it hot from the oven, not even bothering to put butter on it.

Joints of meat could be cooked perfectly by this method, although quite often Grannie Simmons used a Dutch oven for cooking joints and later my Grandmother invariably used the Dutch oven for joints as it was a much quicker process than using the fireplace oven. The best way I can describe a Dutch oven is to ask you to think of a large rectangular tin box lying on its side with an open front. Between the two ends of the box, in the centre, there ran a spindle which was furnished with spikes. The spindle could be turned by a handle on the outside of the box. The joint or bird was then impaled on the spikes and the oven placed on the floor with the open side as near as possible to the fire. From time to time the joint would be turned by means of the handle and it was thus cooked, literally by grilling. The Dutch oven was in fact a smaller, portable version of the old-fashioned turnspit which was used before Elizabethan times. A tray was placed in the bottom of the oven to catch the drippings of fat and gravy. This method of roasting was used by my grandmother until the 1920s.

The ceiling of the kitchen was supported by an oak beam which ran the length of the room from front to rear. In Grannie and Granfer's day this beam was hung with hams and joints of bacon from the pigs which were killed from time to time. There were also a couple of hooks which supported Granfer's muzzle-loading *flintlock gun.* I was never allowed to touch this.

Most of the daily work of the cottage was done on the long wooden table in front of the kitchen window. The surface of the table was always scrubbed white and it was here that we took all our meals. The window embrasure could be used as a seat and it was here I used to sit at mealtimes as it was somewhat higher than the wooden chairs.

Next to the grandfather clock was a small room furnished with a large slate slab. This was the salting room. It was here that the pigs were cut up and the joints salted. Each joint was thoroughly rubbed with *saltpetre* and salt, and this operation was carried out several times until the salt had been well worked into the meat. In those days pigs were bred for fat – practically no streaks of lean meat in it. Rashers of bacon would be cut about a quarter of an inch thick, and fried until they were crisp and golden – and very tasty they were too. No-one had heard of cholesterol in those days and wouldn't have given a damn if they had! Both Granfer and Grannie had lived on a diet of fat meat, butter, cheese and eggs all their lives and both were as lean as beanpoles.

Opposite the front door a stone step led to the back door, and on the left was a small scullery. All water for all purposes was drawn from a well outside the back door, and summer and winter the well was always full of clear spring water. The water was kept in red earthenware pitchers (fig. 52). These came in various sizes from about two gallons down to one quart. Milk was usually kept in these small vessels. These pitchers, although very heavy to handle, were especially useful in summer as their contents always kept very cool.

Figure 52.

Outside the scullery were the steep, angular wooden stairs which led to the two bedrooms, the floors of which were of oak. The wooden beds were furnished with feather mattresses and these were a delight to sleep in, especially on cold nights. The tiny, latticed windows snuggled up under the eaves and looked over the Ambow woods, the entrance to which was about a hundred yards down the road. This wood stretched about a mile and a half in a great arc. I have been told that the area was originally known as 'Hambow' – the wood in the shape of a bow. Time and the Devonshire accent had gradually mellowed this into 'Ambow'. There were nightingales in the wood, and often I have lain in bed listening to their song.

The cottage fronted onto a rough stone path and beyond this the paddock and garden. The path led from the wicket gate up a slope to higher ground and here were situated various small outbuildings, including an *earth closet* which was the only sanitation the cottage boasted. Visitors always fervently prayed that they would never be called upon to visit here during the night, especially if it happened to be raining.

Granfer and Grannie Simmons had only one child – a girl –whom they christened Delilah. Why they chose a name with such unsavoury biblical connections I shall never know. However, it was Delilah who became the mother of my mother – Betty, and the matriarch of the Sowden family. She was always known to me as Grannie Sowden. She married a certain Thomas Nicholls Sowden and they produced eleven children, four boys and seven girls, of which brood mother was the second. This family was born and brought up at Shepton Mallett in Somerset where the father was a prison officer at Shepton Mallett jail. I gathered from my mother that he was a severe disciplinarian and his children received more blows than kind words from him.

> **DELILAH**
> The Biblical Delilah was a beautiful Philistine woman, with whom Samson fell in love. Under her spell, Samson turned his back on the simple ways of his own people, and submitted to her incessant demands to know the secret of his strength. Once Delilah knew that Samson's strength lay in his hair, she betrayed him to her own people, who cut off his hair while he slept.
> *(story from Book of Judges, Old Testament)*

He eventually left the prison service and got a job with the Anglo-Bavarian Brewery at Shepton Mallett, where he proceeded to drink himself to death. On the whole he was looked upon as a bit of an old rip and the family seldom mentioned him. He retired from this life soon after the birth of his eleventh child, Hetty. My father always swore that they sang 'Now Thank We All Our God' at the old man's funeral. Grannie Sowden went to live at Ambow and continued to do so after the death of my great-grandparents. It was during her regime that I spent many holidays there. It eventually became a meeting place and holiday venue for all the Sowden family, their husbands and children as well as a clearing station for news of the family and their offspring, now scattered all over the world.

Chapter 7

The War Years 1914-1918

Figure 53. Denis Cluett's younger brother, Ray

I was seven years old in 1914, the year the Great War began. In the December of that year my brother Ray was born (fig. 53). I have not said much about my brothers but the truth is that I remember very little of them since I was seven years younger than my stepbrother Archie and seven years older than Ray so we always had our own friends and did not play together. In 1914 Archie was apprenticed to a firm of engineers in Tiverton[1] where he lived in digs from Monday until Saturday. When he was seventeen he was called up for the army[2] and was sent to Ireland for training, so he was almost a stranger to me (fig. 54).

The war seemed to make very little impact on the life of the village. I don't think that any of the married men were called up as most of them were either over age or engaged in farming or food production, as was my father. In this war there were no reserved occupations which gave automatic exemption from military service. Everyone was called up sooner or later but if one's employer pleaded that the person concerned was doing a job of national importance a tribunal would decide whether or not the plea was justified (Appendix 6). Most, if not all the young men were called up however, and by 1915 I suppose there were no young men left in the village.

Figure 54. Denis Cluett's step-brother, Archie

1. Stenner & Co., Lowman Ironworks
2. Archie went into the navy in 1919 or 1920

Soon after the beginning of the war rationing was introduced. This was not particularly severe; probably tea and sugar were the worst affected commodities. At the same time an act known as the Defence of the Realm Act, usually referred to as DORA, was passed through parliament. Echoes of this legislation are still with us today in the licensing laws and shop opening regulations (Appendix 7).

I don't know when the first Zeppelin air raids on London took place, but a black-out was introduced fairly soon after the war started. The black-out was not particularly strict but we had to substitute black paper blinds for the buff-coloured linen roller blinds we normally used. The only street lighting we had in Sampford was supplied by a few oil lamps and these had to be dispensed with. The parish employed a lamplighter to look after the street lamps. Every day at dusk he visited each lamp carrying his ladder on his shoulder and a *hurricane lantern* from which he lit the lamps. Next morning he would make the same round refilling the lamps with paraffin and thoroughly cleaning the glass panels and the chimney of each lamp (fig. 55).

I think that the black blinds and the loss of the street lamps were the only outward signs of the war. We had no wireless or television and there was only one telephone (at the post office) which connected Sampford to the outer world. We even set our watches by the church clock and whether this was right or wrong depended upon whether Emma Dunn had remembered to wind it up. Our only regular source of news was the daily paper. The papers were delivered every day as usual and it was not long before the casualty lists began to appear. Every day several columns of the paper would be devoted to printing the names of the killed, missing and wounded and these lists grew longer and longer as the war went on. Only the morning papers were delivered at Sampford but an evening paper 'The Express and Echo' was published at Exeter

Figure 55.

and distributed in Tiverton. If any particularly sensational news broke during the day the Express and Echo would rush out a special edition and a newsboy on a bicycle would be sent out from Tiverton with copies for sale. I still have vivid memories of one such special edition when the newsboy went through the village shouting 'Express and Echo Special! Special! Lusitania torpedoed, great loss of life! Express and Echo, Special! Special!' At the sound of the newsboy's shouts the village suddenly came to life and people dashed from all directions to buy the paper.

Our other main source of news was from the nearest railway station, Tiverton Junction, about 3 miles from the village. The station was on the main GWR[1] Paddington to Plymouth line and was used by the dairy factory for the despatch of butter and cheese etc. The train crews used to spread all the latest gossip and rumour which they collected and disseminated at every station they stopped at. We children often used to walk to the station where we could stand on the platforms and watch the expresses thunder through[2]. Sometimes these trains would be filled with troops and at others they would be packed with the blue-uniformed wounded. All wounded soldiers other than stretcher cases were issued with loose, ill-fitting blue uniforms with khaki shirts and red ties as soon as they reached the country from the fighting points.

In many of the towns and villages men who had not been called up joined an organisation known as the Volunteer Training Corps, the VTC (Appendix 8), where they were supposed to receive some elementary military training. Most of the men in Sampford belonged to this and once a week an ancient retired army captain used to totter out from Tiverton and supposedly teach them the rudiments of drill. Once a month on Sunday afternoons, weather permitting, they went for a route march. The village children did not take these activities very seriously and it was not unusual for them, after Sunday School, to gather on the route of the march where, first ensuring that their lines of escape were clear, they would sing to the hymn tune 'The Church's One Foundation':

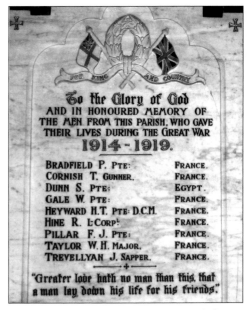

We are the Sampford Army
We are the VTC
We cannot drill, we cannot fight
What bloody good are we?
And when we get to Berlin
The Kaiser he will say
Oh, Gott! Gott! Gott!
What a bloody fine lot
Are the Sampford VTC'

Figure 56. First World War Memorial plaque in St John the Baptist Church

---

1. Great Western Railway
2. It would seem likely that these activities took place at Sampford Peverell Halt - the old station on the site now occupied by Tiverton Parkway Station.

Like every other town and village in the country, Sampford Peverell had its list of casualties. Four or five of the young men of the village were killed (fig.56). When the news of a casualty came through to the village the bell-ringers would assemble at about 8 o'clock the same evening and ring a muffled peal. I always seem to associate these peals with winter evenings; with the rain beating on the windows and the wind tossing the message of the bells from roof to roof and out into the dark countryside beyond.

It was during the war that we moved to the much bigger house which came to be known as 'Tyrella' which I have already described (fig. 57). It was situated on the Tiverton road. Apart from this move our lives and the life of the village seemed to meander along very much as it had always done and most of the war news went over the heads of us children as indeed I expect it did for most of the workers in the fields.

Figure 57. 'Tyrella', the Cluett family home in Turnpike, as it is today

During this period Mother and Father spent a great deal of their time organizing concerts, dances, whist drives etc. for various causes concerned with comforts for the troops. Most of these functions were held in the big assembly hall at the St Boniface Home. I don't suppose it would be permitted to hold any functions in this room today since it was on the first floor and the only means of entrance and exit was a steep flight of narrow wooden stairs. Heaven knows what would have happened had there been a fire, but of course, in those days, there were no complicated regulations and, even if there had been, I don't suppose anyone would have bothered about them at Sampford.

Figure 58. Business advertisement on a matchbox holder

Just above the Canal Bridge in the first house on the Tiverton Road, lived old Harry Wood, the village saddler (fig. 58). One room of his house he had modified by giving it an entrance on to the road and this room he used as his shop and workroom. He was aided in the business by his son and another assistant called Riddler who was inevitably known as Jimmy. In addition to this saddler's business old Harry kept two or three horses, several traps, a governess car and a wagonette (fig. 59) which he used to hire out, with or without a driver, as required. His *ostler* was a married man called Jack Morrell, one of the most cheerful men I have ever met and one of my great friends in the village. Actually Jack was inclined to be a bit eccentric. After the war old Harry acquired a Model T Ford (fig. 60) which he used to hire out with Jack as driver. Jack always treated the car in exactly the same way as he treated the horses. It was not unusual to see the old Ford labouring up the village hill smothered in clouds of steam from the boiling radiator while Jack, with one hand on the steering wheel would lean out of the car and flog the bodywork with a riding crop, at the same time exhorting the vehicle with shouts of 'Come on you old bitch - git up there!'

Figure 59.

Old Harry Wood had mutton-chop whiskers and always wore a skull cap with a tassel on it when he was in the shop or indoors. He was a great believer in the virtue of using tact in all difficult situations. 'Denis, my son' he would often say to me, 'Denis, always remember that you can't beat TACK'. He was one of the stalwarts of the village and, in addition to being a churchwarden, clerk to the parish council and captain of the village fire brigade, he was also inordinately fond of whisky. Before war broke out whisky was 3/6d per bottle and we always used to buy it in one gallon or two gallon stone jars which used to come in wicker casings.

Figure 60.

Every Tuesday a cattle market was held at Tiverton and it was Harry's habit to attend these markets where he could meet the local farmers, collect payments for work done and book further orders for harnesses etc. He always used a governess car pulled by a smart little pony called Charlie for the Tiverton market trip and on arriving at Tiverton would put up at the Prince Regent Hotel (fig. 61). After a walk around the market in the morning he would return to the Prince Regent for lunch and spend the rest of the day in the bar. By almost seven o' clock at night he would often be unconscious, so his cronies would harness up Charlie, tuck up old Harry in the governess car and point the equipage in the general direction of Sampford Peverell. Giving Charlie a good smack on the rump would send him off at a steady trot and he always managed to arrive home in good condition with old Harry snoring his head off in the back. If Harry did not wake up, Charlie would patiently stand outside the front door until somebody came along, usually the village policeman, who would remove Harry from the cart and gently deposit him inside his door (nobody ever locked their doors in Sampford). Charlie would then walk off to the stables where he would await the advent of some good Samaritan who would unharness him.

Charlie was a delightful, high-stepping little pony and was kept only to pull the governess car. This outfit was always referred to as the 'Jingle'[1] because Charlie's harness was decorated with little bells and these used to jingle pleasantly as he trotted around the lanes. Sometimes in summer Mother would hire the 'Jingle' and take three or four of us for a picnic, an activity which I loathed since I always seemed to finish the outing by sitting on an ants' nest or by falling flat on my face into a cow-pat.

---

1. A 'jingle' was also a 'covered 2-wheeled vehicle' (Chambers)

Figure 61. The Prince Regent Hotel, Harry Wood's favourite pub in Tiverton

I have already mentioned that old Harry was captain of the village fire brigade, a position which he held by virtue of the fact that he could always supply a horse and he allowed the fire pump to be housed in one of his barns. The fire pump consisted of a long rectangular box affair which had to be filled with water, usually by buckets from the nearest pump. Beams were mounted, one on each side of the container, and these were pumped up and down by a couple of men to each. In theory this pumped the water through the hoses on to the fire. In practice, however, it did not quite work this way for our fire brigade who had never won honours for putting out a fire. Indeed I never heard of them ever reaching a fire in time to do anything about it. Of course they had a lot of difficulties to overcome. In the first place I don't suppose old Harry would hear about the fire until it had been burning for about an hour. He would then have to harness a horse to the pump and drive around the village environs until he could find enough men to man the machine. Added to this delay was old Harry's insistence, having succeeded in getting his pump fully manned, in taking his crew to the nearest pub for a few rounds of drinks before they started in order to 'keep out the cold'.

The Sampford Peverell fire brigade was not typical of the fire services of that era. I remember once being in Tiverton when the Tiverton fire brigade turned out. This was a magnificent affair. The fire engine consisted of a steam driven pump; the steam being raised by a coal-fired boiler mounted behind the pump. It was drawn by a team of four horses. At the time I saw it, it went through Tiverton's main street with the beautifully groomed horses stretched at full gallop, the driver seated high above them, whipping them on. The black leather harness was superbly polished and glittered with brass decoration. Mounted just behind the driver's seat was a great brass bell which was continually clanged by one of the firemen. On each side of the engine was a long brass rail to which the fire fighting team clung. Every fireman was dressed in blue with brass buttons, topped with well polished thick leather helmets reinforced with highly polished brass. Each man wore black leather boots and carried an axe at his belt.

Once a week during the winter months the Rector held a meeting for the children. These meetings were held in the school and were known as the 'Band of Hope' (Appendix 9), the main theme being the propagation of temperance. Every child who attended the meetings was given a little book which contained all sorts of information and statistics about the evils of drink and these facts were enlarged by the Rector. Every year an examination was held, under the aegis of the Bishop of Exeter, and since I had a knack for absorbing and reproducing facts on paper I used to win a prize every year. These prizes were always books containing the most horrifying and morbid facts about families who had been ruined by the demon drink. The meetings usually lasted about an hour, the first half being given over to the study of our little books. During the second half we were encouraged by the Rector to stand on a chair and give a recitation or sing a song. I used to be one of the regular Sampford 'Bing Boys' and would sing: 'Another little drink wouldn't do us any harm.' (Appendix 3). The parson was delighted with this song and egged me on to sing it every week.

> **BING BOYS**
>
> "The Bing Boys Are Here" was the first in a series of three revues which opened at the Alhambra Theatre in 1916. Over the course of the next two years, it was replaced by "The Bing Boys Are There" (1917) and then by "The Bing Boys On Broadway" (1918); the series ran to over 1000 performances in total. Starring George Robey and Violet Lorraine, "The Bing Boys Are Here" included the famous song 'If You Were The Only Girl in The World', written by Nat D. Ayer with lyrics by Clifford Grey.

Apart from the Band of Hope meetings we children had no incentive for going out during the winter evenings and so we made our own amusement in the house. Most evenings we would pass the time in reading, painting, pasting pictures into scrap books or playing cards, snakes and ladders etc. Sometimes my mother would play the piano and sing or Father would practise conjuring tricks. From time to time visitors would drop in and we would probably spend the greater part of the evening until bed time singing around the piano.

My father had a knack of befriending 'lame dogs' and one of these we all knew as 'Old Tozer'. He was a bachelor of about thirty and quite alone in the world. He lived in digs near Tiverton Junction where he presided over a warehouse and handled the products of a Bristol firm of cattle food manufacturers. It was through this business that my father had come to know him. Nature had endowed Old Tozer with the heart of a child but had been rather rough with him in other respects. His legs were on the short side and tended to bow while his rather outsized feet were encased in black boots above the tops of which his trouser bottoms were encircled with bicycle clips. I never remember seeing him without his cycle clips; even when he came into the house he never removed them. As he walked he leaned forward and peered about him through the thickest pair of pebble glasses I have ever seen. He was always immaculately turned out, from his 2in. [5cm] linen collar to his hair parted meticulously down the middle and plastered straight down on either side. It appears that he had heard Mother sing at a concert somewhere and had expressed himself as being captivated by her voice and was himself a great music lover, so Father invited him to call in for some music and a spot of supper at any time during the winter. Whenever he came he would always produce a roll of dog-eared, very sentimental Victorian ballads from his pocket and get Mother to sing them. His favourite was the sentimental dirge called 'Daddy'. It went like this:

> Lay my head on your shoulder Daddy
> Turn my face to the west,
> It is just the hour when the sun sinks low
> The hour that Mummy loved best. (Appendix 3)

Old Tozer loved this song and would always plead with Mother to sing it. After she had sung the first two lines he always completely stunned those present by falling flat on his face on the hearth rug and bursting into loud sobs.

What with Old Tozer's sobs, Mother fighting to keep her voice steady and the remainder of the company making stifled choking noises as they drank their beer down the wrong way, this ballad was always a great success. After this song was over, those present would pick him up and dust him down and sit him on a chair where he would remain quite quietly until it was his turn to sing. He had only one song and I forget what it was called but the words of the chorus are still with me:

> *Please give me a penny, Sir*
> *My mother, dear, is dead*
> *And oh, I am so hungry, Sir*
> *A penny, please, for bread.* (Appendix 3)

It was a terribly long song all about a young crossing-sweeper of uncertain parentage. As far as I can remember, no-one gave him a penny, so in the last verse he 'handed in his cards', much to everybody's relief, as they made their way to the dining-room to partake of cold meat and pickles.

Meals were rather a formal affair at home; we had to appear properly dressed and with washed hands and faces. The worst part of mealtimes was that after we children had finished we had to watch the adults leisurely finishing the meal while we were dying to leave the table and go out to play. On occasions, however, the peaceful atmosphere of the meal would be suddenly shattered. Mother and Father both loathed wasps and if one appeared in the middle of a meal chaos would erupt. Both parents would leap to their feet and, grabbing the nearest implement to hand, would prepare to do battle. It was a heartwarming sight to watch Father brandishing a carving knife while Mother rushed around the opposite way brandishing a soup ladle. The remainder of those present usually took avoiding action by getting under the table. Eventually the wasp would either escape through the window or come to an undignified end in a plate of soup. Victory having been achieved we would immediately resume our seats and continue the meal with our usual imperturbable decorum.

Figure 62.

Stainless steel cutlery had not yet been invented and all table knives had to be cleaned by rubbing with the dampened end of a cork which had been dipped in brick-dust. Some time towards the end of the war we acquired a mechanical knife cleaner (fig. 62) consisting of two felt pads enclosed in a cast iron container with a handle at the top by which the top pad could be rotated. Some brick-dust was sprinkled between the pads, two or three knives inserted between, the handle turned like mad and, Hey presto! one removed two or three beautifully polished knives. After continued polishing, these knives would acquire razor-sharp edges and one always had to take care when handling them.

> **KNIFE CLEANING**
> The brick dust used for cleaning knives was scraped from 'bath bricks', which were made in Bridgwater especially for this purpose. The dust was used as a scouring powder, which was also used to clean steel fenders and to scour floors.

Like most, if not all, of the village children I had two suits of clothes: one for weekdays and a best suit for Sundays. With our suits we usually wore white *Celluloid collars* which had to be fastened to the front and rear of the shirt neckband with studs. The advantage of these collars was that they could be cleaned by wiping them over with a damp cloth. I personally never wore a hat except on Sundays, especially in summer, when I was made to wear a white Panama hat secured under the chin by an elastic band. Quite a lot of the younger boys wore sailor suits on Sundays and I can remember (I suppose I was about five) going to church dressed in a white sailor suit topped with a Panama hat which sported a black silk ribbon around the crown with the legend HMS Victory in gold letters impressed upon it.

It was not considered to be quite the done thing for adults to wear Celluloid collars and the majority of non-manual workers wore white linen collars. These took quite a lot of laundering as not only had they to be boiled, washed and starched in the usual way, but before ironing they had to be rubbed very thoroughly with some waxy substance, the name of which escapes me. This had the effect of bringing up a very smooth shiny finish. Cuffs of white shirts also had to be prepared in the same way, as these were worn stiff. It was possible to buy false shirt fronts and false cuffs which were sometimes worn by an adult if he did not possess a white shirt.

Neither men nor women were ever seen out of doors without a hat. As far as men were concerned their choice of hat was usually confined to a bowler, a cloth cap or a soft felt hat known as a trilby. In the summer men often wore a hard straw hat known as a boater (fig. 63). This hat was normally decorated with a black band around the crown, but if one belonged to a club, possibly a cricket club, it was quite usual to substitute a band in the club colours for the black one. Schoolboys' boaters would usually sport their school colours. The boater was a light hat and was easily whipped from the head by a sudden gust of wind so it was usual to attach a silk cord to the brim by means of a clip while the other

Figure 63.

end of the cord could be clipped into the button-hole in the lapel of the jacket.

Ladies often wore boaters and, like all ladies' hats, they were worn with a veil. These veils were of fine silk mesh and often patterned. They were secured over the brim of the hat and pulled down over the face. The veil was then tightened by twisting the end under the chin. When paying an afternoon call ladies never removed their hats or their veils and even if they were invited to afternoon tea they would simply lift their veils just high enough to sip a cup of tea or nibble a sandwich.

At the beginning of the war ladies wore their skirts with the hems almost touching the ground but as the war went on the hemlines began to rise until, by 1918, they were being worn three or four inches above the ankle. As time went on one saw more and more ladies riding bicycles but in order to protect their modesty they

---

LADY WALROND
She was the wife of the Honourable Lionel Walrond, Conservative M.P. for Tiverton from 1906 to 1915, and President of St Boniface Home for Waifs and Strays. The couple lived at Bradfield House, Uffculme.
'Following in his father's footsteps, Lionel Walrond entered parliament, although it was his wife, Lottie, who stole the limelight on the local political platforms – on occasions lifting her skirt to prove her drawers were the right colour!'
Extract from Culm Valley Album, by Anthony Taylor

---

would clip a length of black elastic to the skirt hem and attach the other end to the shoe. This ensured that the skirt did not blow up in the wind and expose their calves to the gaze of the vulgar. I remember a terrific furore being caused in and around the village by a certain Lady Waldron [sic] who lived at a place called Willand about four miles away. She was a young woman and was on most of the fund-raising committees in the area. Towards the end of the war she attended one such committee at Sampford, and after the business of the meeting had finished she hitched her skirt to the top of her calves and perched on a corner of the table where she actually crossed her knees and lit a cigarette. The effect on the committee members was tremendous and the story of this fast and reckless behaviour swept through the village like a prairie fire. The women of the village spoke of the matter in horrified whispers while their menfolk fought like mad to try and get appointed to the committee.

My recollections of ladies' fashions are very hazy but I do remember the very large hats some of them wore, often decorated with artificial flowers and even artificial fruit. In order to keep them in place when out of doors they thrust long steel hat pins through the hat and into their piled-up hair. Summer and winter they always wore gloves when they went out; these were usually of kid or wash-leather, while in summer they would substitute ones of white cotton or cotton net. If a woman was in mourning she would, of course, wear black gloves.

Watches were often hung from a gold or silver chain around the neck and attached to the blouse, brooch fashion. As far as little girls were concerned their one great day of the year was Whit Sunday when, if it was humanly possible, their mothers would provide them with new dresses and long

---

OAK APPLE DAY – MAY 29TH
"The 29th of May is Oak Apple Day. If you don't give us a holiday, we'll all run away". *(Children's rhyme)*
The Anniversary of the return to England of King Charles I and the monarchy was celebrated for 200 years. Although the Public holiday was abolished in 1859, children continued to celebrate. Those not wearing oak apples would have their bottoms pinched; hence the day also became known as Pinch Bum Day!

---

white cotton stockings. Thus adorned, they would proudly parade to church and Sunday school. The boys were not so fortunate. We only got a new pair of knickers when the backsides had been repaired so often that there was insufficient cloth left to which any more patches could be attached. Most of the lads were fitted with breeches which had been cut down from an old pair of corduroys discarded by the father.

In addition to Whitsun there were two other days in the year marked by the children. The first of these was Palm Sunday when we all wore buttonholes of catkin buds and the other was the anniversary of the reputed date when King Charles I hid in an oak tree from his pursuers. On this date we always wore oak apples in our buttonholes or caps.

It was not until after the war that bicycles (fig. 64) became more common in the village. Up until this time none of the children ever possessed one and only one or two of the adults. Tricycles could still be encountered on the roads. These were usually ridden by dignified old gentlemen clad in *deerstalker* hats, Norfolk jackets and knickerbockers (fig. 65).

Figure 64.

I think most of the villagers could read and write, although they usually found the latter rather a labour. Many of them came to my father for assistance in any bits of

business in which they might find themselves involved. Thus it was that he came to be looked upon as the local legal expert and general confidant by most of the villagers. One of those for whom Father had a particularly soft spot was one Jim Milton. Jim had worked on a farm all his life from the age of 12 and up to 1914 his weekly wage had never exceeded 7s.6d. He must have been about 60 when we knew him. He and his wife Anne lived in a little 'one up and one down' candlelit thatched cottage at the top of the village.[1] He suffered from some kind of spinal defect which caused him to be bent almost double when he walked. He always wore a

Figure 65.

---

1. The 1901 Census shows James Milton, aged 53 (i.e. 68 in 1916) living at Norrish's Cottages (see map) with his wife Annie Mary, aged 70 (i.e. 85 in 1916)

battered old bowler hat, green with age, and an old 'cutaway' coat which had once been black but was now as green as his bowler hat. His outfit was completed by the usual pair of corduroys, hitched up to just above the tops of his hobnail boots and a red and white spotted handkerchief knotted around his neck. He invariably carried a sack over his shoulder, the contents of which always remained a mystery.

Just before the end of the war Anne Milton died and on the eve of her funeral Jim asked Father to visit his cottage. On arrival there he found Anne's coffin resting on trestles in the kitchen. The lid was in place but had not been screwed down. Seated at the coffin and using it as a table sat Jim eating his supper by the light of a candle. Arranged before him on the coffin top was a huge crust of bread and cheese flanked by a pot of pickled onions and a mug of tea. I think Father must have registered some slight surprise when Jim poured out another mug of tea and invited him to pull a chair up to the coffin and join him in a bit of supper. "Doan yew worrit about Anne yur,' said Jim, 'er niver 'urt nobody when 'er was livin' so 'er won't do us no 'arm now 'ers daid."

After supper Jim confided that he and Anne had saved a bit of money and now that Anne had gone and the cottage would be empty all day he would like my father to look after it for him. Thinking that the savings would probably be five or six pounds, Father agreed to this so Jim went upstairs. After a time he came back with his arms full of bags and tin boxes and proceeded to empty these onto the coffin. By the light of the flickering candle Father proceeded to count the money and, to his utter amazement, counted out nearly two hundred pounds - all in pennies, threepenny pieces and sixpences. Naturally Father was not at all keen to hold himself responsible for this sum and persuaded Jim finally that the money should be put into the bank. Jim agreed that this should be done, but he took a lot of persuading since he didn't fancy his money being in the hands of strangers and I don't suppose he had ever heard of a bank anyhow.

So it happened that on the day after the funeral Father took Jim into Tiverton to visit the bank. Jim watched intently as his money was passed over the counter and checked by the cashier who then made out a deposit account slip and handed it over. Jim suspiciously examined the slip from every angle. He looked at my father and then examined the slip again. "Is this all oi gits?" asked Jim. He was assured that the slip was all that was necessary. "In that case," said Jim, "Oi'll 'ave me money back." My father tried to explain. The cashier tried to explain. Several junior clerks came forward and tried to explain, followed by the Assistant Manager, aided by several kindhearted customers with time on their hands (almost everyone had time to spare in those days). All tried to give him a rundown on the banking system. Eventually, after the bank's business had been brought to a complete standstill for the best part of half an hour, Jim finally capitulated on the understanding that Mr

Cluett should visit the bank once a week and count the money. Father and the bank staff all promised faithfully that this should be done and Jim suffered himself to be taken home.

Jim went on working until the end of the war but then recurrent bouts of rheumatism grew more and more frequent and he had to stop. Father discovered that he had a niece living at Burlescombe, a village about five miles away. She proved to be a kindly woman and agreed to have Jim in her home until he died. He had expressed a wish to be buried beside Anne at Sampford, so for his funeral he was brought back to the village, his coffin jammed upright between the front and rear seats of old Harry Wood's Model T Ford, his niece seated beside him. So Jim, who had never walked upright in his life, travelled home to Anne as erect as any guardsman.

I think the two oldest people in the village were a couple called Mr and Mrs Gardiner; I never heard their Christian names[1]. They were both well over 90 years of age and lived in considerable neglect and poverty in what had once been a prosperous farmhouse (fig. 66). Mother used to send them hot lunches and sometimes it fell to my lot to deliver the tray. I was always frightened to death by this job. The house was dark and gloomy and always dead silent. I had to walk in without knocking and traverse a long dark hall until I came to the kitchen. There I would find the couple

Figure 66. Trucklegate Cottage, Uplowman, as it is today

1. Almost certainly Philip and Sarah Gardiner at Trucklegate, Uplowman. In 1916 they would have been 86 and 81 respectively. Presumably Denis would have been driven there in a pony & trap or horse & cart.

sitting upright and silent on wooden chairs. Both looked incredibly old. The old woman always wore a mob cap like Queen Victoria and the old man had a full beard which tumbled down over his chest and appeared to be matted with the overspills of long forgotten meals. Their wrinkled faces were ingrained with dirt; neither of them had had a wash for years. When I entered the kitchen to deposit my loaded tray on the cluttered table I was aware of their eyes following my every move, but neither of them ever spoke to me. I never lingered; I was only too glad to get out of the house without having had a spell of some sort put upon me.

The couple had, at one time, been very prosperous farmers, but they had been overtaken by ill luck. Whether this was due to bad husbandry or the wretched state of farming at the time I don't know. To add to their troubles all their cattle began to die. They were convinced that someone had put a curse on them so the old man set off to walk eighteen miles to visit the white witch of Exeter (Appendix 10) who had a wonderful reputation for her ability to lift curses. The old man saw her and, after exacting her fee, she gave him a small leather bag and enjoined him to hang it around his neck and to wear it day and night. This he did, but it appeared to have no effect upon their fortunes since all their cattle died and they ended up practically penniless.

When his wife died the old man became quite incapable of looking after himself so Father approached Emma Dunn who agreed to give him a home in her cottage for a few shillings a week. So one afternoon the old man was duly conveyed to Emma's cottage by horse and cart. About an hour later Father decided to go along to see if the old man had settled in comfortably. On knocking at Emma's door he got no reply so he went in and walked through to the back yard where he was confronted by the old man, as naked as a baby, standing up to his knees in a tin tub of hot water while Emma scrubbed him down with a stiff-bristled, long-handled yard brush and liberal applications of red carbolic soap. The old chap soon died and after his death Father rescued the witch's bag from his body and found it contained some bones from either a small animal or bird, a piece of animal fur and a small piece of paper on which were written some indecipherable signs.

The war dragged its weary way into 1918 and although our community at Sampford missed its worst effects, yet it hung over the village like a cloud. When the armistice came in November the villagers, in their usual phlegmatic way, did not go in for any wild celebrations. Strangely, all that I can remember of that dull and drizzly November 11th was a hastily arranged dance held in

---

THE END OF THE WAR
Extract from School Log Book
November 11th 1918
Yesterday the abdication of the Kaiser was announced. Today at noon the news came that fighting ceased at 11am, - an armistice having been signed with Germany. After singing the National Anthem etc, the school was dismissed till Wednesday (13th) morning.

the St Boniface Home hall. I suppose, although no-one knew it at the time, that dance marked the end of an era for the village. It certainly marked the end of an era for me because the following Easter I went away to school (fig. 67)[1] and from that time saw the village only during my holidays.

Figure 67. Denis, aged about 17, in West Buckland School blazer

1. West Buckland School, North Devon – see Appendix 11

Glossary

avoirdupois
an imperial system of weights in which the pound (lb) equals 16 ounces (oz)

bay rum
an aromatic liquid made from the leaves of the bayberry tree (Pimenta acris) and used medicinally and cosmetically

billycan
a lidded cylindrical metal container, with a wire handle, used for boiling water, cooking etc over an open fire out of doors

black leading
the process of blacking grates by applying the black mineral, plumbago (graphite)

Blakey's Boot Protectors
shaped rubber reinforcing strips, nailed to soles of boots or shoes at toe and heel

brilliantine
a liquid hair dressing for making the hair glossy

cachou
a sweet with extract of liquorice, used to sweeten the breath

camphorated oil
used to relieve irritation of the skin

carbolic soap
obtained from coal tar

Celluloid collar
a spongeable collar made from an early form of plastic

copper
a boiler, originally made of copper, for washing laundry

Culmstock Beacon
At 250m above sea level, Culmstock Beacon was one of a series of beacons, which was lit to signal the sighting of the Spanish Armada in 1588. The blazing fire beacon was also the signal for all able-bodied men to assemble at the local church, await instructions, and arm themselves

deerstalker
a hat with peaks at the front and back and flaps at the side that can cover the ears

dubbin
a preparation of grease for softening or proofing leather, especially boots

earth closet
an outdoor privy in which solid wastes are covered with earth

fender
a guard, often made of brass, surrounding the hearth to confine falling coals and ashes.

firkin
originally a measure equal to a quarter of a barrel (9 gallons of liquid or 56 pounds of butter). The term also came to be used for a smaller portable container for liquids, especially beer or cider

flintlock gun
a hand gun or musket, in which flint, struck by a hammer, produces sparks which ignites the gunpowder

French knitting
'French knitting' uses a cotton bobbin with four pins or small nails in the top, around which wool is looped with a crochet hook. The 'knitting' subsequently appears through the hole in the bobbin as a 'tube'

hurricane lantern
a lamp so made as not to be extinguished by the wind

magic lantern
a simple apparatus for projecting pictures on slides on to a screen

mantle
fragile fireproof covering of a gas jet, which produces a brightly glowing light

ostler
a person in charge of stabling horses, originally at a coaching inn

pantry
a small room or cupboard where food, plates, cutlery etc are stored

passing bell
a bell tolled immediately after a death, originally to invite prayers for the soul passing into eternity

pauper
a destitute person, supported by charity or public provision

pediculosis
lousiness, usually head lice

privy
a lavatory, usually in its own shed or outhouse

quill
the hollow basal part of a bird's feather; also the whole of a large feather, especially that of a goose - formerly used for making pens

rabies
an acute viral infection that is nearly always fatal. Rabies in humans is usually transmitted by dogs. Animal rabies was eradicated in Britain in 1922. The last human death from rabies in the UK was recorded in 1902

range
an enclosed kitchen fireplace fitted with facilities for heating water and cooking food; a forerunner of Rayburns and Agas

Romany
a gypsy; a member of a wandering people of Indian origin

saltpetre
potassium nitrate, used as a preservative

scullery
a small room attached to the kitchen for washing dishes etc

sprig
a headless or almost headless nail

suet
the solid fatty tissue which accumulates around the kidneys of oxen, sheep etc, used in making sweet and savoury boiled puddings

voluntary
an improvised composition of any kind; usually a piece of music played before, during or after a church service

vorelock
forelock of a pony or horse; also the lock of hair left at the front after a 'short back and sides' man's haircut. Touching one's forelock was a mark of respect when meeting one's 'superior'.

R.S. NORRISH & SONS LTD

The business started in 1884 at Fordlands Farm, Chevithorne, the home of Mr R.S. Norrish. He purchased milk or cream from farmers in the surrounding area to be made into butter which was sold under the trade names of "Devonshire Girl" and "Farmer's Boy" brands of "best butter". The business expanded and in 1899 a factory was established at Sampford Peverell, trading as R.S. Norrish and Sons Ltd, managed by Mr W.H. (Bill) Norrish.

At that time all milk was delivered to the factory by horse and cart. The milk was separated and the by-products were either returned to the farmer or used for feeding pigs. During the 1914-1918 war products being manufactured were: butter, cream cheese (apparently not rationed), Cheddar, Caerphilly and 'Household' cheese. The latter was a skim milk cheese with a high acid and moisture content giving a crumbly texture and having a short shelf life.

After the War a lorry was purchased which was driven by Mr Harry Lovell, and shortly after this a second lorry was driven by Mr Ernest Gunn, whose wife worked at the dairy. The business grew during the 1920s and 1930s and the number of lorries increased eventually to seven, collecting milk from about 150 farms in 12- or 17-gallon churns, and at peak the intake was around 2000 gallons per day.

The Company was bought out in 1940 or 1941 by Aplin and Barrett of Yeovil who also had a factory at Mantle Street, Wellington. All the milk processing was transferred to Wellington and the factory at Sampford Peverell was retained as an emergency creamery. The managing director during the last few years was Mr Clifford White, a relative of Mr Bill Norrish. The Norrish family home was almost adjoining the factory in what is now the Merriemeade Hotel.

Source: *"The Transition from Tradition to Technology: A History of the Dairy Industry in Devon"* by **Peter Sainsbury**

ST BONIFACE HOME FOR BOYS

This home for boys was one of several owned by The Church of England Waifs and Strays Society. Between its foundation in 1881 and the end of the First World War, The Waifs and Strays Society cared for around 22,500 children. It opened its first home at Dulwich in 1882 and by 1918 it had run nearly 175 homes all around England and Wales. Some of the homes were open for a few years, while others operated for decades. The Waifs and Strays Society became the Church of England Children's Society in 1946 and is now known as The Children's Society.

St Boniface Home was opened in 1907, using existing buildings vacated by the East Devon County School. It could house up to sixty boys, aged between seven and fourteen, who were sent there from all over the country. The boys attended the local school and wore uniforms that distinguished them from the other children. Out of school-time, the boys were kept busy with such activities as carpentry, gardening and gymnastics.

It was particularly well supported by the Sampford Peverell community, as is evidenced in the local newspapers of the time. Donations were individually acknowledged at frequent intervals in the papers, listing the donors and their gifts. These ranged from such items as a penny for every child, to a few shirts and larger sums of money raised by special collections. At Christmas-time, the list of gifts included several donations of oranges and figs as well as cards for every boy.

The Home continued in operation until 1952; subsequently the buildings were demolished and the site was re-developed for housing as part of Court Way.

Source: www.hiddenlives.org.uk

WORDS OF SONGS

Denis Cluett seems to have enjoyed singing – to judge by his clear memories of the songs sung at School and by the farm labourers – and he sang regularly in his later school life at West Buckland (see Appendix 11). The words that follow - of the less familiar of the songs referred to in the text - are redolent of a bygone age:

"LET THE REST OF THE WORLD GO BY"

With someone like you, a pal good and true,
I'd like to leave it all behind, and go and find
A place that's known to God alone:
Just a spot to call our own.

We'll find perfect peace, where joys never cease
Out there beneath the kindly sky.
We'll build a sweet little nest, somewhere out in the West
And let the rest of the world go by.

1919. Words by J. Keirn Brennan; Music by Ernest R. Ball

"ANOTHER LITTLE DRINK (Wouldn't Do Us Any Harm)"

Oh, there was a little hen and she had a wooden leg,
The best little hen that ever laid an egg,
And she laid more eggs than any hen on the farm,
And another little drink wouldn't do us any harm.

We had a little duck and a lot of green peas,
A quart of ginger beer and some Stilton cheese,
Then we felt such a pain in the shade of the palm,
And another little drink wouldn't do us any harm.

I went to a ball dressed as a map of France,
Said a girl: "Show me how the French advance",
When she reached the firing line I shouted in alarm,
And another little drink wouldn't do us any harm.

1916. Words by Clifford Grey; Music by Nat. D. Ayer

"THERE'S A LONG, LONG TRAIL A-WINDING"

Nights are growing very lonely,
Days are very long;
I'm a-growing weary only
Listening for your song.
Old remembrances are thronging
Thro' my memory.
Till it seems the world is full of dreams
Just to call you back to me.

Chorus:
There's a long, long trail a-winding
Into the land of my dreams,
Where the nightingales are singing
And a white moon beams:
There's a long, long night of waiting
Until my dreams all come true;
Till the day when I'll be going down
That long, long trail with you.

All night long I hear you calling,
Calling sweet and low;
Seem to hear your footsteps falling,
Everywhere I go.
Though the road between us stretches
Many a weary mile.
I forget that you're not with me yet,
When I think I see you smile.

Chorus:
There's a long, long trail a-winding...

1915. Words by Stoddard King; Music by Alonzo "Zo" Elliott

"DADDY"

1
Take my head on your shoulder, Daddy,
Turn your face to the west;
It is just the hour when the sky turns gold,
The hour that Mother loves best.

2
The day has been long without you, Daddy,
You've been such a while away;
And now you're as tired of your work, Daddy,
As I am tired of my play.

3
But I've got you and you've got me,
So everything seems right;
I wonder if Mother is thinking of us,
Because it's my birthday night.

4
Why do your big tears fall, Daddy?
Mother's not far away.
I often seem to hear her voice
Falling across my play.

5
And it sometimes makes me cry, Daddy
To think it's none of it true,
Till I fall asleep to dream, Daddy,
Of home, and Mother and you.

6
For I've got you and you've got me,
So everything may go;
We're all the world to each other, Daddy,
For Mother, dear Mother, once told me so.

7
I'm sometimes afraid to think, Daddy,
When I am big like you,
And you are old and grey, Daddy,
What you and I would do

8
If, when we got up to Heaven
And Mother was waiting there,
She shouldn't remember the two she left
So sad and lonely here.

9
But year by year still seems no change,
And so 'twill all be right;
We shall always meet her in our dreams.
Daddy, good night; Daddy, good night,
Dear Daddy, dear Daddy, good night, good night.

1890. Words by Mary Mark Lemon; Music by Arthur Henry Behrend

"O WHO WILL O'ER THE DOWNS SO FREE"
(Hickenstirn's Song) *see note below*

O who will o'er the downs so free,
O who will with me ride,
O who will up and follow me,
To win a blooming bride?
Her father he has lock'd the door,
Her mother keeps the key;
But neither door nor bolt shall part
My own true love from me!

I saw her bow'r at twilight grey,
'Twas guarded safe and sure,
I saw her bow'r at break of day,
'Twas guarded then no more!
The varlets they were all asleep,
And none was near to see
The greeting fair that passed there
Between my love and me!

I promis'd her to come at night,
With comrades brave and true,
A gallant band with sword in hand
To break her prison through:
I promis'd her to come at night,
She's waiting now for me,
 And ere the dawn of morning light,
I'll set my true love free!

Words and Music by Robert Lucas Pearsall (1795 – 1856)

Note: In the North aisle of St Michael's Church, Winterbourne, Gloucestershire, is a monument to Hugo de Stunden (Hickenstirn), whose elopement in the 14th Century with the heiress of the Bennetts of Syston Court is celebrated in the above song.
("The History of Winterbourne" by H.W.N. Ludwell)

"PLEASE GIVE ME A PENNY, SIR"

1

Please give me a penny, Sir,
My mother dear is dead,
And oh! I am so hungry, Sir,
A penny, please, for bread.

2

All day I have been asking,
But no one heeds my cry;
Will you not give me something?,
Or surely I must die.

3

Oh! please give me a penny, Sir,
My mother dear is dead,
And oh! I am so hungry, Sir,
A penny please for bread.

4

Please give me a Penny, Sir!
You won't say "no" to me,
Because I'm poor, and ragged Sir,
And oh! so cold, you see.

5

We were not always begging;
We once were rich like you,
But Father died a drunkard,
And Mother – she died too.

6

Oh! Please give me a penny, Sir,
My mother dear is dead,
And oh! I am so hungry, Sir,
A penny please for bread.

7

"Please give me a penny, Sir"
Is heard on every side,
Lisped by little trembling lips,
Singing on Life's tide.

8

Oh! Listen to their pleadings
And pity these the poor.
Then blessings brought from heaven
Will shine on thee the more.

9

Oh! please give me a penny, Sir,
My mother dear is dead,
And oh! I am so hungry, Sir,
A penny please for bread.

1870. Words and Music by William Seibert

Appendix 4

POSTMISTRESS'S DOWNFALL

An account of the trial of Miss Taylor can be found in the Tiverton Gazette dated 6 November 1917 and reads as follows:

'**Devon Assizes opened at Exeter on Friday before Lord Coleridge.**
Maud Taylor, 40, postmistress at Sampford Peverell, was charged with fraudulently converting to her own use £132.6s.5d., belonging to the Postmaster General; also with making a false entry in the cash account. She pleaded 'Guilty' to both offences. Mr. Parry, prosecuting, said the accused had been postmistress at the sub post office since May 1, 1915. In May 1917, the postmaster of Tiverton, in making the audit found a deficiency of £132.6s.5d., which had arisen since the last audit in November 1916. The postmaster asked for an explanation, but the accused hopelessly failed, being, in his words, 'stupefied and ill'. Counsel said the stupefaction and illness were due to whisky. The woman's fall was, in fact, attributable to drink. It was clear that money had been taken out of the till to pay for an inordinate quantity of whisky.
His Lordship said the frauds were serious and bore traces of design. They could not be attributed to inability to keep the accounts or to accident. Twelve months' imprisonment in the second division.'

The committal proceedings had been reported in great detail in the same newspaper two months earlier. These reveal some additional information. Charles Ponsford, a temporary postman, said that on many occasions when people went into the post office for money, there was none in the till and Miss Taylor had sent to various people in the village to borrow some! The same witness added that Miss Taylor would send out almost every day for a noggin or a noggin and a half of spirit, at a cost of about 5s. to 6s; it was easy to understand where the money went. There is, however, no mention of any possible involvement by Bert Cornish. Consequently, 'the general opinion in the village that he was the real culprit' appears to have been completely groundless.

Appendix 5

COURT CASES OF PC BLACKMORE
(Police Constable Alfred John Blackmore)

In writing that he "..had never been known to make an arrest", Denis Cluett was doing PC Blackmore rather less than justice. The following selection of cases in which he was involved, culled from the pages of the Devon & Somerset News, gives an idea of the level of crime prevalent in Sampford Peverell at the time. Dates refer to the issue of the newspaper in which the case (heard usually at Cullompton Petty Sessions) was reported.

13.2.1913-**Philip Lodge**, a tramp, sentenced to 10 days' imprisonment for begging. ("The prisoner called at the local constabulary and asked PC Blackmore to lock him up. The constable replied that he could not, whereupon the prisoner said he should, and then begged from the constable")

24.7.1913-"**George Trevelyan**, labourer, summoned for stealing a quantity of timber, value 5s., from Joseph Salter, proprietor of The Globe Inn". After much questioning of the accused and PC Blackmore, the case was eventually dismissed.

22.1.1914-"**Walter Kerslake**, of Uffculme, pleaded guilty to not keeping a horse and cart under control at Sampford Peverell. PC Blackmore stated that the horse was left on the highway with no-one in charge for twenty minutes. Fined 7s.6d."

30.4.1914-"**William Mitchell Browne**, medical practitioner, summoned for keeping a motor car without a licence". Among other excuses, Dr Browne pleaded ignorance of the law and the case was closed by the Chairman saying "The Bench have decided to let you off on payment of costs – 6s."

30.7.1914-**John Cottrell**, slaughterman, summoned for riding a bicycle without a light. "I didn't know it was so late". Fined 5s.

21.1.1915- **William Williams**, platelayer, summoned for using obscene language at The Globe Inn. "When asked [by PC Blackmore] to be quiet, defendant sneeringly said "It's a long way to Tipperary". Defendant was under the influence of drink at the time. Fined 8s.6d.

13.5.1915-**Ida Goffin**, 55, and **Theresa Trevelyan**, 30, married, pleaded guilty to stealing wood, value sixpence, the property of Stanley Williams, butcher. Fined 10s. each.

8.7.1915-**William Henry Norrish**, of The Creamery, summoned for not keeping a dog under control. "PC Blackmore gave evidence as to finding the dog straying about midnight. Defendant said really the dog belonged to the firm of R.S. Norrish, Ltd, of which he was [only] a trustee." Fined 10s.

MILITARY TRIBUNALS

The Devon & Somerset News regularly reported the results of Military Tribunals set up to consider applications for exemption from military service. Most of those relating to Sampford Peverell men appear in 1916, with one as late as 1918:

Sampford Creamery Staff "H.J. Lovell, 33, married, dairy engineer for Norrish & Sons and W. Cluett, 36, married, secretary and managing clerk for the same firm: Military assented to the latter, but did not think Lovell was indispensable. Mr Norrish said 9 out of 14 had joined voluntarily, and [the Company] had not appealed for any of them; these were replaced by women and boys and old men. The military assented to exemption for Mr W.H. Norrish, managing director of the firm"
(**D. & S. News, 25.5.1916**)

Percy Bradfield, assistant master of St Boniface Home. "The Committee applied for postponement." The master (Mr Keeley) was temporarily absent, having been wounded at the Battle of Loos. The Chairman "...thought the proper course would be for the master to come back when he had recovered, and take charge of the Home, so that the younger man Bradfield could go." Postponement agreed.
(**D. & S. News, 10.2.1916**)
His subsequent death (from wounds sustained in action) was reported in the D. & S. News of 8th November 1917: "...an impressive memorial service was conducted...by the Rev. J. Rees".

John Henry Morrell, "...described as a horseman, looking after five horses for Mr Henry Wood, who wrote that he had failed to find a substitute. The military did not assent to postponement, and did not consider the man indispensable. A member [of the Committee] remarked that plenty of odd job men could be got to do this work, and the Tribunal refused the application."
(**D. & S. News, 10.2.1916**)

Stanley Williams, "...aged 24, married, proprietor of retail butcher's shop...claimed absolute exemption on grounds of 'national interest' and 'certified occupation'. Military did not assent; civil occupation no longer necessary in the national interest. The Chairman suggested that Mr Williams' father might run the business while this applicant was away on military duty, for despite his years he was a very active man. The military assented to two months' exemption."
(**D. & S. News, 30.3.1916**)

Frederick William Taudevin, grocer, draper, etc. (aged 44): The Military had appealed against an earlier decision by a local tribunal to allow him two months to make arrangements for his business to operate in his absence. The Chairman dismissed the military's appeal, on condition that Mr Taudevin agreed not to apply again for exemption. Mr Taudevin agreed, saying: "I am not so much concerned to evade military service as to get time".
(Devon & Somerset News, 4.7.1918)

There is also an entry in the School Log Book for May 16th, 1916, indicating that the Assistant master, Mr Moyse, "...left school at 11.00 a.m. to [attend an] interview [at] the Tiverton military tribunal". The outcome is not recorded.

DEFENCE OF THE REALM ACT (DORA)

The **Defence of the Realm Act (DORA)** was passed in the United Kingdom on 8th August 1914, during the early weeks of World War I. It gave the government wide-ranging powers during the war period, such as censorship and the power to requisition buildings or land needed for the war effort.

Some of the things the British public were not allowed to do included: flying a kite, lighting a bonfire, buying binoculars, feeding bread to wild animals, discussing naval or military matters and drinking alcohol on public transport. Alcoholic beverages were themselves watered down.

DORA ushered in a variety of authoritarian social control mechanisms, including some that are still in use today, such as British Summer Time, which was enacted in May 1916 as a device for boosting wartime production.

The first person to be arrested under DORA was John Maclean, a Marxist and Clydeside revolutionary, for uttering statements deemed to be prejudicial to Armed Forces recruitment. He was fined £5, but he refused to pay and spent 5 nights in prison.

Source: www.wikipedia.org

VOLUNTEER TRAINING CORPS

A Volunteer Force was formed during the Great War for Home Defence. From 1914 to 1916 a body called the Volunteer Training Corps was raised and administered privately with the recognition of the War Office, but in 1916 the War Office authorised the raising of Volunteer Units under the Act of 1863, and the existing Corps thereafter came under the control of the War Office.

A new Act was passed in 1916, which gave effect to agreements on the part of members of the force to undergo military training or to perform military duties (or both), and rendered such members subject to Military Law. From May 1918, men granted exemption certificates under the Military Service Acts were liable to serve in the Volunteer Force as a condition of exemption from compulsory service in the Army. The training they received meant that they would have some military experience already, if and when they were released by their employers to join the armed forces.

No details of the Sampford Peverell unit appear to have survived, but the Uffculme detachment was very active from early 1915, if not before, and, from reports in the Devon & Somerset News, often included VTC members from Sampford in their activities. At the invitation of the Rector (Rev. J. Rees), they visited Sampford Peverell for a church parade on Sunday, 28 March 1915, at which the Rector said that there was "…a call at the present serious crisis for all to do something to show their manliness…England wanted, today, men in whom the current of life was strong, men who would stand by a righteous cause, come what might"
(D & S News, 1.4.1915)

Other contemporary reports from the Devon & Somerset News include:

"The Uffculme Volunteer Training Corps, including a contingent from Sampford Peverell, were inspected…by Colonel Kirkwood, officer commanding the Devon Regiment… Col. Kirkwood said "…I am very pleased with the Uffculme Detachment. I consider that they have done their very best, and are showing by their conduct that whatever they can do they are ready to do… What is wanted now is duty by everybody…I want you to tell your friends that young men are wanted…"
(21.10.1915)

"The little Culm Valley town of Uffculme has from the start of the movement been an enthusiastic centre in support of the Volunteer Training Corps, and now musters over fifty members, including a small detachment from Sampford Peverell. The Drill-hall, which was completed shortly before the war, has been a useful place for assembly, drill and indoor shooting, but the need of an outdoor range was much felt, and the Uffculme Parish Council was approached for permission to make such a range at Uffculme Down. This was readily given, and early in May the members set about doing the work themselves... On Saturday the range was ready for opening, and the Hon. Mrs Walrond, of Bradfield, graciously officiated and fired the first shot, scoring a bull." **(13.7.1916)**

THE BAND OF HOPE

Founded in the industrial city of Leeds in 1847, The Band of Hope was the first temperance society exclusively for children. At that time, social and working conditions were appalling - such that many people, including children, sought release from their misery by the consumption of alcoholic drinks. Based on Christian principles, the Society required all its members to take 'The Pledge' of total abstinence from alcohol. Regular meetings were held throughout the country at which the 'evils of drink' were taught, songs were sung and the children entertained by magic lantern slide shows (invariably also with a temperance theme).

Having moved its Headquarters to London, the organisation grew and grew until by 1900 it had over three million members in twenty-six thousand local branches throughout the United Kingdom. Sampford Peverell was one of these branches, being one of the most active in the Diocese of Exeter.

In 1917 and 1918 Denis Cluett was one of around fifty children from Sampford Peverell who took the Church of England Temperance Society examinations. In both years he qualified for an individual prize; in the second year he achieved the highest marks amongst his peers. Sampford Peverell won the 'Michelmore' Challenge Banner in both years, which was awarded to the parish with the highest aggregate marks.

The disruption caused by the two World Wars saw the demise of the Band of Hope, which like so many similar organisations struggled to adapt to the 20th century. However, its modern descendant, Hope UK, remains with the purpose of helping to care for children with drink and drug problems.

Sources:
1. The Exeter Diocesan Temperance Journal. (May 1917 and May 1918 editions).
2. "The Hope of the Race" by Robert Tayler, published by Hope Press, 1946.

"THE WHITE WITCH OF EXETER"

We have not succeeded in positively identifying this individual (nor where in Exeter she was to be found) but there are some references in contemporary records.

The North Devon Journal of April 25th 1907 relates the "...remarkable story of a farmer who journeyed from Ilfracombe to Exeter to see 'the White Witch' respecting the death of three horses. The animals had died in a mysterious manner...Two veterinary surgeons were unable to say what ailed the animals, and after the death of the third, the farmer decided to consult "the White Witch". This woman visited the farm and told the man he had undoubtedly been witched". Presumably she lifted the curse (no doubt at a price!) because "...in answer to the interrogation as to whether he really believed in the superstition, he replied, definitely, that he was sure it was right, adding: "And 'twas a good job I went, or else I should have lost everything. I lost all my horses, and 'twas awful! – awful!"

An earlier story, from Dalwood, near Axminster, concerns an old woman named Mother Dark who "...was suspected of causing the illness of a cow, a fact confirmed by a White Witch of Exeter, whom the farmer consulted. The White Witch promised to make Mother Dark suffer as she had made the farm animals suffer, and soon afterwards the old woman was admitted to hospital, suffering from a mysterious illness. Her ailment coincided with the end of the epidemic on the farm."

And from "Devon & Cornwall Notes & Queries, Vol. 4 (1906-1907):
"A seventh son, in Exeter, was reputed to be a witch. Someone with a wound to the arm was given a small velvet amulet to wear, which was believed to contain the leg of a toad".

So perhaps the bones in old Mr Gardiner's bag were those of a toad. We shall never know!

DENIS CLUETT AT WEST BUCKLAND SCHOOL

Denis entered West Buckland School, near Barnstaple, in May 1919. It was then a boys-only boarding school of some 170 pupils. Over the years it expanded, and at the start of the school year in September 2006 there were about 700 pupils (boys and girls) of whom about 100 were boarders, with 200 or so in the preparatory section.

Denis was assigned to Courtenay House (the others being Grenville, Brereton and Fortescue). He was above average academically, winning prizes for: 'General Work' and Maths & Science; the Carter English prize in 1924 and 1925 and the Divinity prize in 1925. He played a very full part in the extra-curricular life of the school. He attained the rank of corporal in the Officer Training Corps and was a member of the School Shooting Team, gaining his 'colours' in 1925.

He was a prominent member of the School Debating Society and is commended in several of the Society's annual reports for his contributions to debates, one of which was on the motion "This house deplores the tendency of women to usurp the manners and modes of men". Denis spoke for the opposition!

It is clear from his reminiscences that Denis derived much pleasure from singing (both at school in Sampford Peverell and in church) and this is reflected in his regular appearances – albeit always in the chorus – in the annual school productions of Gilbert & Sullivan operettas. He was also a member of the West Buckland School Choir.

Denis Cluett left West Buckland School in December 1925, having stayed an extra term to re-take part of the Cambridge School Certificate.

Source: *West Buckland School Archives*